The Music
Library

The History of
American Folk Music

The Music Library

The History of American Folk Music

By Adam Woog

LUCENT BOOKS
A part of Gale, Cengage Learning

GALE
CENGAGE Learning

Detroit • New York • San Francisco • New Haven, Conn • Waterville, Maine • London

Thanks for research advice to Hugh Blumenfeld.

© 2006 Gale, a part of Cengage Learning

For more information, contact
Lucent Books
27500 Drake Rd.
Farmington Hills, MI 48331-3535
Or you can visit our Internet site at gale.cengage.com

LIBRARY OF CONGRESS CATALOGING-IN-PUBLICATION DATA

Woog, Adam, 1953–
    The history of American folk music / by Adam Woog.
        p. cm. – – (The music library)
    Includes bibliographical references (p.   ) and index.
    ISBN 1-59018-734-2 (hard cover : alk. paper) 1. Folk music – – United States – – History and criticism – – Juvenile literature. I. Title. II. Series: Music library (San Diego, Calif.)
    ML3551.W66 2006
    781.62'13009 – – dc22   2005037809

Printed in the United States of America
5 6 7 12 11 10 09 08

• Contents •

• Foreword •

In the nineteenth century, English novelist Charles Kingsley wrote, "Music speaks straight to our hearts and spirits, to the very core and root of our souls. . . . Music soothes us, stirs us up . . . melts us to tears." As Kingsley stated, music is much more than just a pleasant arrangement of sounds. It is the resonance of emotion, a joyful noise, a human endeavor that can soothe the spirit or excite the soul. Musicians can also imitate the expressive palate of the earth, from the violent fury of a hurricane to the gentle flow of a babbling brook.

The word *music* is derived from the fabled Greek muses, the children of Apollo who ruled the realms of inspiration and imagination. Composers have long called upon the muses for help and insight. Music is not merely the result of emotions and pleasurable sensations, however.

Music is a discipline subject to formal study and analysis. It involves the juxtaposition of creative elements such as rhythm, melody, and harmony with intellectual aspects of composition, theory, and instrumentation. Like painters

mixing red, blue, and yellow into thousands of colors, musicians blend these various elements to create classical symphonies, jazz improvisations, country ballads, and rock-and-roll tunes.

Throughout centuries of musical history, individual musical elements have been blended and modified in infinite ways. The resulting sounds may convey a whole range of moods, emotions, reactions, and messages. Music, then, is both an expression and reflection of human experience and emotion.

The foundations of modern musical styles were laid down by the first ancient musicians who used wood, rocks, animal skins—and their own bodies—to re-create the sounds of the natural world in which they lived. With their hands, their feet, and their very breath they ignited the passions of listeners and moved them to their feet. The dancing, in turn, had a mesmerizing and hypnotic effect that allowed people to transcend their worldly concerns. Through music they could achieve a level of shared experience that could not be found in other forms of communication. For this reason, music has always been part of religious endeavors, from ancient Egyptian religious ceremonies to modern Christian masses. And it has inspired dance movements from kings and queens spinning the minuet to punk rockers slamming together in a mosh pit.

By examining musical genres ranging from Western classical music to rock and roll, readers will find a new understanding of old music and develop an appreciation for new sounds. Books in Lucent's Music Library focus on the music, the musicians, the instruments, and on music's place in cultural history. The songs and artists examined may be easily found in the CD and sheet music collections of local libraries so that readers may study and enjoy the music covered in the books. Informative sidebars, annotated bibliographies, and complete indexes highlight the text in each volume and provide young readers with many opportunities for further discussion and research.

"Music That Falls Between the Cracks"

It's all folk music to me. I ain't heard no horses playing it.

—attributed to jazz trumpeter Louis Armstrong and blues singer Big Bill Broonzy, among others

Sometimes, defining folk music is relatively simple. Traditional folk music is anonymously written music from a given culture or heritage. It is performed by "folk"—the ordinary people in the community—usually on acoustic instruments. And it is transmitted aurally—that is, learned informally through hearing and repetition, not through written notation; as folklorist Alan Jabbour notes, this makes it "person-to-person music in a participatory style."[1]

Defining American folk music, however, is trickier. The category is so richly diverse that no single style alone is American folk music. Some experts disdain the phrase "American folk music" completely, preferring "roots mu-

sic" as a nod to the genre's complex, intertwined sources. One of the key figures in American folk music, Mike Seeger, calls it simply "music that falls between the cracks."[2]

"One More Reason"

Several reasons underlie American folk music's slippery nature. For one thing, America is a nation of immigrants. Native Americans created the country's first folk music, joined in time by the musical traditions of each new group of immigrants. These traditions stayed relatively pure and isolated from one another for a long time, but eventually they began to influence each other.

As the country expanded, remarkable musical traditions also grew from groups connected by bonds of work, not necessarily by ethnicity. Among them were sailors, lumberjacks, railroad workers, and the pioneers and cowboys of the West. What is today considered "American folk music" thus began as a

"The Rhythm of Ordinary Life"

Folk music, especially American folk music, is incredibly diverse and rich. Writer Phil Hood comments:

Folk music is the rhythm of ordinary human life—a constant source of inspiration, amusement, and diversion in every race and culture. It is campfire entertainment and religious sacrament, a call to arms, and a witness against injustice. It is a spiritual legacy and connection from one generation and one age to another. It is love songs, and drinking songs, and wedding songs, and nursery rhymes, and gospel hymns, and funeral laments, and patriotic songs that make a whole country sing with one voice. It is stomps, and field hollers, and dirty blues, and gentle waltzes, and that high and lonesome sound. It is the hardy original species of music, from which all the flashier hybrids are cultivated.

Phil Hood, ed., *Artists of American Folk Music*. New York: Morrow, 1986, p. 4.

mix of music from many countries, cultures, and work environments.

The Strands Intertwine

Another factor complicating the definition of American folk music is that today it encompasses much more than the "real" folk music of the old days. More than a century and a half ago, professional songwriters began composing in the style of old folk songs. Old and new quickly mingled together and, to the general public, became virtually interchangeable. One example is a nineteenth-century favorite, "Carry Me Back to Old Virginny"; few people knew that it was not an anonymous folk song but the work of an African American professional songwriter, James A. Bland.

The line between traditional folk and other genres, including commercial pop music, continued to blur. This was especially true in the early decades of the twentieth century, when radio and records revolutionized how people heard music. Previously, folk music had been more or less restricted to small, isolated groups, with relatively little outside influence. Now, however, new worlds opened up as commercial pop music came to remote parts of the country—and as traditional folk, in turn, influenced commercial pop.

Distinctions between folk and other genres were further eroded by singers who merged traditional folk with songs about political issues. This reached new heights with the folk revival of the 1950s and 1960s. The social and political turmoil of those times, created by such issues as civil rights and the Vietnam War, inspired the rise of a style called protest music. Singers and composers like Pete Seeger, Woody Guthrie, Bob Dylan, and Joan Baez played music that was not strictly folk, but that owed a great deal to the folk tradition, to passionately address a variety of political issues.

The definition of American folk music expanded to include this new development. In the years since, the music has continued to evolve and change, influencing and being influenced by shifting tastes in the music world.

Each wave of immigrants brought its own musical tradition to America. This diversity helped shape American folk music.

While traditional ethnic folk music is still very much a part of it, American folk today includes much more as well. Writer David Hajdu notes, "There never was one single American folk music, of course, but rather a loose clump of threads extending from Appalachian mountain, hillbilly, cowboy, rural blues, urban blues, union, left-wing propaganda, military, hobo, and other kinds of music, intertwined and knotted."[3]

"Real and Living"

This rich musical stew, in all its permutations and quirks, is today recognized as one of the country's most valuable national treasures. Folklorists John A. Lomax and Alan Lomax remark that American folk musicians "have created . . . a heritage of folksongs and folk music equal to any in the world."[4] This extraordinary body of music continues to serve as an inspiration for new generations of performers.

As a result, American folk music is far from dead. Instead of being something found between the dusty pages of a book or in museum-piece re-creations of ancient songs, folk continues to change in new and sometimes surprising ways. As musicologist B.A. Botkin notes, "Folklore is not something far away and long ago, but real and living among us."[5]

The roots of this extraordinary music lie far in the past, and two ethnic groups played especially important roles. White settlers from the British Isles—England, Scotland, Ireland, and Wales—brought ancient traditions of dance music and vocal songs, which later developed into such sophisticated forms as bluegrass. Particularly important was the great wave of Gaelic—that is, Scots-Irish—settlers that arrived in the latter part of the 1600s. Folklorists Roger D. Abrahams and George Foss note of this group that "their spread throughout North America established the dominant language, song style, and repertoire for white rural America."[6]

Meanwhile, African slaves and their descendants created songs of their own, for worship and other purposes. These songs eventually were called spirituals; in time, the spirituals evolved into the blues and other powerful folk genres. These two traditions, black and white, form American folk music's twin foundations, as folk song historian Oscar Brand notes: "American folk music . . . owes its existence to immigrants from every country in the world. But it was the Briton and the African who, above all, fashioned our national songbag and gave the rest of the world one more reason for envying the American people."[7]

Chapter One

British Folk in the New World

More than any other nation, America has had the fertile soil from which the seeds of "people music" could grow in abundance.

—music historian Samuel L. Forcucci,
A Folk Song History of America

In the 1600s, when the first white colonists arrived in America, folk music of the British Isles was already hundreds of years old. As with any folk tradition, its exact beginnings cannot be dated with certainty. However, it was clearly ancient; many tunes familiar to the colonists can be traced back at least to the mid-1400s.

Because this music had developed over several centuries, by colonial days it was richly varied. Regional differences accounted for much of this variation. Scottish tunes, for instance, were quite distinct from those of Ireland, Wales, or England, and there were clear regional differences within smaller divisions of these lands.

Nonetheless, folk music of the British Isles overall shared certain characteristics. For instance, a given tune typically fell into one of two categories. It was either an instrumental dance tune or an unaccompanied vocal song.

Instrumental Music

Instrumental music was primarily for dancing. As in most cultures, dancing was a major form of entertainment for the working class that typified the early British immigrants. It was nearly always part of the festivities whenever communities of farmers or other laborers gathered. (Members of the British aristocracy had their own, highly stylized dance music.)

The instruments used to play British folk dance music were varied. Some were simple and inexpensive, such as the pennywhistle, a staple of Irish music. Others were relatively sophisticated, such as bagpipes—both the famously loud Scottish variety, powered by a bladder filled by the performer's lungs; and the softer, melancholy Irish variant, the uilleann pipes, which used a bladder held under the musician's arm.

However, far and away the most common instrument for dance music was the fiddle, as folk musicians typically called the violin. The fiddle remained popular as the first immigrants traveled to America. It was sophisticated enough to handle any melody from the most delicate to the most lively; but it was also small and could be carried on a difficult ocean voyage or while creating a home in a rugged new country.

Types of Dance Music

There were many styles within the broad category of dance tunes. One of the most common was the reel—a fast-paced dance, usually performed by couples, typically in 2/4 time and with a distinctive "da-diddle-da-diddle-da-diddle" rhythm. Among the most familiar reels were lively tunes like "Mairi's Wedding" and "Toss the Feathers."

A group of immigrants plays its instruments in a tavern. A common and popular folk music instrument is the fiddle.

Another common type of dance tune was the jig. Jigs were brisk solo dances; the music was usually in a triple time signature (such as 6/8) with a "diddley-diddley-diddley" rhythm. The tune "Cherish the Ladies" is typical of the hundreds of jigs from the Irish-British tradition.

Still another common dance tune style was the strathspey. Strathspeys were slow, stately dances from Scotland, usually played in 2/4 or 4/4 time; their melodies featured syncopated ornamentations (short added notes that briefly shift the melody away from the regular beat) called

This engraving from the 1500s depicts couples dancing outdoors in England.

Scottish snaps. A classic example of a strathspey is "The Bonnie, Bonnie Banks of Loch Lomond."

Singing Solo

The second basic category of British folk music was the vocal song. Traditional British singing had strict rules. First, it was almost always performed solo. (There were some exceptions, notably the choral singing of the Welsh tradition.)

The ways in which British folk songs were performed were also very particular. Songs were almost always performed *a cappella*—that is, without instrumental accompaniment. The singer used a high-pitched, nasal, and often mournful voice. The vocal cords were typically kept tight, which made the performance intense rather than relaxed.

Furthermore, it was important to stay close to recognized, traditional performances. Straying too far from a known, familiar melody was unacceptable. Improvisation or embellishment—a crucial element in the music of other cultures—was not important.

This emphasis on performing songs in the same way, passing them from one generation to the next, created a sense of continuity. Songs became a part of a group's shared history, and the singer was essentially an oral historian, taking a secondary role to the music itself. Abrahams and Foss note, "The singer views himself as a voice for whatever piece he is performing; he places himself in the background, letting the piece speak for itself."[8]

Francis Child documented several hundred ballads during the 1800s that still exist today.

Ballads

There were many overlapping subgroups of vocal song. One prevalent form was the ballad, which, simply put, told a story. This was usually an exciting tale of legendary figures, great lovers, or famous battles. Ballads were full of drama, romance, and melodrama, and they often included a hefty dose of supernatural elements such as witches and spells.

The core of the traditional repertoire consisted of several hundred key songs. Today about three hundred examples of these so-called root songs still exist; they are called the Child ballads, in honor of Francis Child, a nineteenth-century American musicologist who collected,

The Devil's Music

Not everyone approved of the widespread use of fiddles in the British folk tradition. To them the fiddle represented ancient associations between music and the devil. Some deeply religious groups thus considered the instrument, and the dances it was used for, wicked and irreligious. To them dance tunes were "the devil's music"; further-more, the devil was the king of the fiddle and the primary teacher of fiddlers. These beliefs were ancient; stories about the gift of music coming from supernatural creatures such as fairies or about people being the devil teaching someone to play in the graveyard at midnight existed for many centuries in Europe before white settlers came to America.

documented, and classified them. Among the best-known Child ballads are "Barbara Allen," "The Cruel Mother," "The House Carpenter," and "Lord Rendal."

The simple melody, repeated lines, and lack of variation in these Child ballads made them easy to pass on orally from one generation to another. The songs thus significantly helped people (who were often illiterate) preserve moments in their collective history. Musician and music historian Hugh Blumenfeld notes, "Set to music, important stories—even long ones—could be remembered and passed down from one generation to the next, learned simply by repeated hearing and singing."[9]

Lyric Songs

Among the other types of typical British folk songs brought to America were lullabies, nonsense songs, and the large category called lyric songs. Generally speaking, lyric songs did not focus on storytelling. Instead, they expressed universally felt emotions like love, grief, and humor.

Some lyric songs are dialogues. For example, in "The Devil's Nine Questions" a series of riddles must be answered correctly; if not, the devil says, the answerer will belong to him. (The song ends when a clever girl answers them correctly.) Other lyric songs are essentially monologues, such as the expressions of enduring love sung by the performer in "The Banks of the Roses."

Work Songs and Broadsides

Some traditional songs were used while working. For example, immigrants from Scotland, especially the Hebrides Islands, used "waulking songs." These highly rhythmic songs were used by groups of weavers to keep their rhythms synchronized as they stamped or pounded on cloth to tighten the weave.

Sailors had their own work songs, called chanteys or shanties. These were also highly rhythmic, helping groups stay together while performing repetitive tasks such as hauling in lines. One well-known example is "The Coasts of High Barbary" and its frequent repetition.

Yet another type of song, the broadside, was not a traditional folk song but was related. Broadsides were satirical or topical verses set to familiar tunes. Broadsides were printed and sold on the street, exceptions to the general rule that songs were passed on orally.

Broadsides first appeared in the sixteenth century and remained popular in England and colonial America. These early forms of protest music were called

A choir sings religious hymns without instrumental accompaniment in this 1700s woodcut.

"singing newspapers" because of their topicality. Music professor Samuel L. Forcucci notes that they were not just entertaining but informative as well: "Broadsides were an important and powerful vehicle for the efficient and widespread dissemination of news."[10]

Religious Music

Early American settlers also sang songs of worship. (Some groups of colonists, in fact, forbade any music other than religious music.) The primary place for religious songs, of course, was in church. But people also sang them at home and in camp meetings. Typically held in temporary tents, camp meetings featured several days of continuous services and were part of the massive religious movements that swept America in the late eighteenth and early nineteenth centuries.

Music was a powerful draw at these religious meetings. People especially enjoyed singing songs that used familiar tunes (such as folk tunes) but had new, religious lyrics. Because of this, the line separating folk music and religious music was sometimes indistinct.

Preachers typically doubled as song leaders, teaching the music to their congregations (who were generally lacking in musical technique). A simple call-and-response system called "lining out" was used. The minister sang a line and the congregation repeated it in unison—that is, everyone singing the same melody, with no harmony.

A more sophisticated technique was shape note singing. (It was also called Sacred Harp singing, after the title of a popular songbook of the mid-1800s.) The shape note method involved a simplified musical notation, using different symbols to represent notes. By looking at the shape, singers knew which note to sing.

Shape note singers typically used three- or four-part harmony, but had no instrumental accompaniment. The resulting sound was spare and plain, but also vigorous and beautiful. Though the shape note tradition waned in New England in the early nineteenth century as people there increasingly learned standard music notation, it continued to thrive in the Midwest and South through the 1800s.

Isolated

The earliest colonists had settled along the Atlantic seaboard. As time went on, many remained in bustling coastal cities like New York and Boston. However, many others chose to move farther west and south, exploring the land's wilder regions. In particular, many settled in the beautiful but isolated Appalachian Mountains. Successive waves of settlers continued farther, in particular into remote regions of the Ozark Mountains and the Deep South.

These settlers had only the most rudimentary roads connecting them with each other and the outside world. Days of arduous travel on horse or foot were needed simply to go from one community or farm to another. Families thus grew accustomed to fending for themselves—and this, of course, included making their own entertainment.

A Multitude of Uses

The traditional folk song can have many different uses. Singer and writer Theodore Bikel reflects:

A folk song does so many things. It tells a multitude of stories, legends, fables, and jokes. It admonishes, lulls to sleep, calls to battle, rings with hope for the prisoner, with threat for the jailer, with joy for lovers, and with bitterness for him who might have had but didn't. It heralds birth, boyhood, wedlock. It soothes the weary, the sick, and the aged, and it mourns the dead.

Quoted in Ronald D. Cohen, *Rainbow Quest: The Folk Music Revival and American Society*, 1940–70. Amherst: University of Massachusetts Press, 2002, p. xii.

Because of their isolation the music these people played remained relatively free of outside influence. There were no radio shows or big-city performers to introduce new songs. There were no phonograph records or radio broadcasts to influence playing styles.

As a result, successive generations played and sang the ancient songs in much the same ways as they had learned them. The Scottish immigrants who typified settlers in the Appalachians were classic examples. Blumenfeld notes, "Because of their love of music, their fierce nationalism . . . , and because of their geographical isolation, these Scottish immigrants maintained a relatively pure musical tradition."[11]

Alterations

The music did not stay entirely pure, of course. Sometimes words or melodies were misheard or poorly remembered, just as messages are changed in the children's game of repetition called Telephone. Sometimes new ballads were created out of whole cloth. One of the first ballads to be composed entirely in America, for example, was "The Death of General Wolfe," commemorating a hero killed in 1759 during the French and Indian Wars.

Sometimes old melodies were fitted with new lyrics. A famous example of this was the British national anthem, "God Save the Queen," which in the hands of rebellious colonists became "God Save the Thirteen States." Later, the same melody was used for "America" (the patriotic song that begins "My country, 'tis of thee").

Performance styles also sometimes changed. For example, Appalachian fiddlers typically played their instruments "incorrectly," resting them on their chests rather than under their chins. Another characteristic of Appalachian fiddling was its highly rhythmic "saw-stroke" technique, which used shorter and more powerful bow strokes than earlier British musicians had used.

String Bands

Over time British folk music in America began to change in other ways as well. In particular, dance music became more sophisticated. For example, several instruments, rather than a single fiddle, became the norm for dance music.

This development came about with the widespread adoption of the banjo and guitar. The banjo was originally an African instrument brought to America by slaves. White settlers liked its bright sound and loud volume, and a number of regional variations developed, such as Kentucky style (using the thumb and first finger) and North Carolina style (which used three fingers). Meanwhile, the guitar—an import from Europe— also found favor as a rhythmic accompaniment to fiddle tunes.

Traditional string bands used the guitar, banjo, and fiddle as their main instruments.

The fiddle, banjo, and guitar together formed a string band—arguably the first true group performers of American folk music. String bands sprang up all over America in the late 1800s. They became familiar sights at dances, at parties, or simply on front porches.

Songs of the Pioneers

By this time settlers were no longer inhabiting just the eastern part of the continent. New generations and new immigrants were continuing to push westward, settling the frontiers of the Great Plains and the West. Naturally, they took their traditional music with them—and they created new songs as well.

A body of highly distinctive songs developed as pioneers settled these new regions. Musically these tunes were generally rooted in traditional British music, but lyrically they reflected the experiences and daily lives of the people who invented them. They illustrated the hazards of travel in wagon trains or exploring the wilderness; they told tales of bad weather, illness, rugged country, and dangerous animals; they described great battles or dramatic love affairs.

Some songs were playful, like "Skip to My Lou" (a *lou* was a sweetheart,

Pictured is a handmade five-string banjo from the 1800s.

derived from the Scottish word for "love"). Others were lullabies, like "Hush Little Baby." And many were associated with the miners of the 1849 California Gold Rush, such as "Oh, Susanna" and "Darlin' Clementine."

One of the most famous pioneer songs is "Sweet Betsy from Pike." This lively tune tells the tale of a motley group (including two yoke of oxen, a big yellow dog, a tall Shanghai rooster, and one spotted hog) crossing the country with brave Betsy in the lead.

American Music

Gradually, as the country itself grew, several strains of homegrown American music were developing. In some cases British-derived folk was being preserved more or less intact. In other cases, such as the development of string bands and the songs of the pioneers, it was developing in distinctly new and original ways.

Meanwhile, less conspicuously but no less importantly, another strain of indigenous folk music was brewing. This was the music of the African American tradition as performed by slaves, ex-slaves, and their descendants. It was the second main root system of folk music in America.

In America slaves accompanied themselves with instruments similar to those they were familiar with, making them from materials at hand. For example, they cut lengths of cane to make fifes, a type of flute. However, this was often severely curtailed, because many slave owners banned their use of instruments—especially drums.

The ban on drums was a question of control. In Africa drums were frequently used to communicate over long distances, and slave owners often feared that groups of slaves isolated on farms or plantations could use them to share information about rebellions. Writing of Caribbean slaves in the 1680s, one observer, Sir Hans Sloane, noted, "They formerly on their Festivals were allowd the use of Trumpets after their Fashion, and Drums. . . . But making use of these in their Wars at home in Africa, it was thought too much inciting them to Rebellion, and

Africans dance to a drumbeat in the 1800s. In America and the Caribbean slave owners banned the use of drums among the slaves.

A Lively Service

The worship services of black slaves were typically very lively. This passage is by a visitor to one such service in 1820:

After sermon they began singing merrily, and continued, without stopping, one hour, till they became exhausted and breathless. "Oh! Come to Zion, come!" "Hallelujah, &c." And then "O won't you have my lovely bleeding *Jasus!*," a thousand times repeated in full thundering chorus to the tune of "Fol de rol." While all the time they were clapping hands, shouting and jumping, and exclaiming, "Ah Lord! Good Lord! Give me *Jasus!* Amen."

Quoted in Eileen Southern, *The Music of Black Americans: A History.* New York: Norton, 1997, p. 78.

---

so they were prohibited by the Customs of the Island."[14]

New Elements

Because of this ban, slaves usually made music using little more than their voices and "body percussion"—hand claps, foot stomps, and knee slaps. Nonetheless, they continued to honor tradition as best they could. Musicologist Alan Lomax notes, "Few African instruments survived in North America, but African musical habits did."[15]

These habits were passed on long after the first generation of slaves died. However, as the old African languages were gradually forgotten, songs were increasingly performed in English. This change was only one aspect of how African American music developed during this period—an aspect that illustrated a dramatic difference between black and white folk traditions.

British musical tradition prized keeping the music "pure" by reproducing ancient songs exactly. The African tradition was just the opposite. It stressed individual expression, improvisation, and the introduction of new elements.

Improvisation

Slaves thus frequently created variations on old melodies and lyrics or invented entirely new ones. They freely borrowed elements from existing songs, refitting them with new melodies or words or using pieces of two old songs to make a single new one. Furthermore, performances of a given song were often radically different every time, since singers were encouraged to put individual stamps on even familiar songs.

Slaves adapted or invented songs for many different reasons. Some were for simple domestic situations, such as lulling babies to sleep. Some were just fun to sing (an example is "Shortnin' Bread"). And, of course, slaves had work songs called "field hollers." These helped lift spirits, pass the time, and, as with traditional British work songs, helped coordinate group activity by using frequent repetition.

Religious Song

Another especially important reason for slaves to sing, as with their white masters, was to express a deep religious faith. The first slaves had brought with them religious songs traditional to their ancestors. However, in America another religious influence became increasingly powerful: the Christian faith of their masters.

Although in some cases Christianity was forced on unwilling slaves, most slaves were powerfully attracted to it. Its promise of a better life to come offered hope to those who lived in wretched and oppressive conditions. Its declaration of the equality of all before God was also deeply moving. And the Bible's simple, powerful stories—of Moses delivering the Jews from bondage or of Jonah regaining freedom through faith—had clear parallels in the slaves' daily lives.

Christian beliefs thus began mixing with those from Africa, and the slaves' adoption of Christianity profoundly affected their music. These seemingly disparate worlds began to combine and make something new. Music historian Dena J. Epstein notes: "One can hardly overstate the importance of conversion to Christianity [among] blacks in the New World. . . . African religious beliefs and musical practices undoubtedly continued to make their contribution, [but they] combined and intermixed with Christian doctrine to form a distinctive and universally appealing body of song." [16]

Jubilee Songs

From this merger of Christian and African sensibilities came a large and varied group of anonymous folk songs. These songs had a variety of names, including corn ditties, cornfield ditties, and jubilee songs. They reflected both the lives of the slaves and their belief in a better world, as the African American composer James Weldon Johnson noted in 1929: "The Negro took complete refuge in Christianity, and the [songs] were literally forged of sorrow in the heat of religious fervor." [17]

Many jubilee songs had double meanings. Some held coded messages associated with the Underground Railroad, the network of whites and free blacks that helped southern slaves flee the South. For example, the lyrics of "Follow the Drinking Gourd" helped escapees maintain a northward course toward freedom.

Other songs with double meanings were not such practical codes; rather, they were expressions of both religious salvation and freedom from slavery. "Go Down, Moses," for instance, compared the plight of black slaves with the biblical story about the enslavement (and eventual freedom) of the Jews by exhorting a master to "let my people go."

Changes

Some jubilee songs were newly invented, but many were adapted from European hymns. For example, "Roll, Jordan, Roll" can be traced back to a Methodist hymn by a well-known British composer, Charles Wesley (who in turn borrowed the tune from a song celebrating a naval victory).

Slave congregations felt free to change the hymns they sang. They altered lyrics, adding extra verses or using different words. They also added distinctive musical touches from the African tradition, such as call-and-response singing and strong polyrhythms. Even the basic melodies of hymns frequently changed, as singers improvised using such techniques as bends, slurs, or slides.

This woodcut depicts an African American church congregation in the 1870s. Many slaves adopted Christianity and integrated Christian traditions with their own religion and music.

The Fisk Jubilee Singers created a new style of music, the spiritual, by blending jubilee songs from the days of slavery with classical music from Europe.

All of this was markedly different from the European singing tradition, as was the way in which slaves physically produced sung notes. Traditional British folk singing used a closed throat and tight vocal cords to produce an intense and high-pitched sound; the African style, by contrast, used an open, relaxed throat to produce a sound that was deeper and, to use a modern term, more soulful.

Spirituals and the Fisk Jubilee Singers

Jubilee songs were widely sung by slaves all over the South in the early part of the nineteenth century. The mu-sic was all but forgotten, however, in the immediate aftermath of the Civil War, which ended in 1865 and resulted in the end of slavery; no ex-slave wanted to recall those hated years. Nonetheless, within a decade the songs re-emerged in changed form.

One group was primarily responsible for this surge in popularity: the Fisk Jubilee Singers, a student choir from Fisk University in Nashville, Tennessee — one of the first American universities established specifically for black students. The Fisk singers performed jubilee songs, but with the rough edges smoothed over by elements of European classical music. This new blend of styles had a name: the spiritual. Broadly speaking, spirituals were songs rooted in slave music but formalized with "correct" European harmony, notation, and accompaniment.

The heyday of the Fisk singers marked the first time that black American folk music was heard and appreciated by large audiences outside of the South. The group's audiences, who were mostly white, loved its dignified but heartfelt renditions of spirituals. The Fisk singers' enormously successful tours in America and abroad earned a fortune for their school, spawned several rival groups, and attracted such admiring fans as Queen Victoria of England, U.S. President Ulysses S. Grant, and author Mark Twain.

The Blues

As the twentieth century dawned, another important style of black folk music was emerging: the blues. Blues songs expressed both the hardships and pleasures of life, its deeply felt pain and its joy—or sometimes a bittersweet mixture of the two. Though influenced to a degree by the British ballad tradition, the blues was most closely connected to African American religious song. Blues guitarist Johnny Shines once remarked, "Church music and the blues is all one and the same. They come out of the same soul, same heart, same body."[18]

Musically, the early forms of the blues were fairly simple. A typical blues song was built on a plain but sturdy framework: It had a twelve-bar rhythmic structure—that is, each verse had twelve measures in 4/4 time—and its chords formed a basic I-IV-V progression. The lyrics set to this framework were catchy, repetitive, and earthy.

The use of "blue" or "bent" notes in the melody lines, meanwhile, gave the blues an especially plaintive and expressive feel. Frequent embellishments in the style of spirituals—swoops, slurs, shouts, and other techniques— added to the music's power. In the hands of the right performer, the blues could be by turns terrifying, seductive, heartbreaking, or hilarious.

Singing and Playing the Blues

No one can pinpoint the exact birth date of the blues. Scholars generally agree that it began developing sometime in the late 1800s or early 1900s. Nor can its precise birthplace be found, although it undoubtedly began in the South. The fertile Mississippi River delta is often acknowledged as the cradle of the blues, but a number of other regions, such as Louisiana and the Piedmont region of North Carolina, also developed distinctive blues styles.

The instruments used to accompany a blues singer were simple, cheap, and often homemade—perhaps a guitar, a harmonica, a jug to blow into, or a bass made from a washtub, a broomstick, and a length of rope. In those days before amplification, the National steel-body guitar, with its loud, bright tone and built-in acoustic amplifier, was especially popular. Over time, performers invented new ways to make these various instruments sound fresh. For example, a bottleneck or knife blade, when slid over guitar strings, produced a suitably eerie and mournful sound; the notes of a harmonica could also be bent to create blue notes.

During the formative years of the blues, its single most important figure,

Musician Robert Johnson (pictured) set the standard for early blues.

Robert Johnson, set a daunting standard for every performer who followed. According to legend, Johnson made a pact with the devil at the crossroads in Clarksdale, Mississippi; in return for his soul, the story goes, Johnson was given the ability to play and sing better than anyone.

Johnson's life and death also served as a template for the classic bluesman. After a hard, fast life and a handful of haunting recordings, Johnson died in 1938, still in his twenties. He was probably poisoned by a girlfriend or a girlfriend's jealous husband.

Mixing It Up

For centuries the folk music of white and black Americans had remained more or less separate. There were exceptions, such as slaves who were taught European instruments like the fiddle and piano. In general, however, it was rare for a black musician to play white music or vice versa.

By the first decades of the twentieth century, this well-defined line was beginning to blur. For example, the classic British ballad form was evident in many songs from the black community. One instance was "John Henry," the story of a legendary "steel-drivin' man" who worked on the railroad; another was "The Titanic," a moving narrative of the famous disaster.

The reverse—that is, the influence of black music on white performers—was also becoming increasingly common. White musicians had enthusiastically adopted the banjo, for instance, and

Dwelling Side by Side

Over time, the separate black and white streams of folk music began to influence each other. This blurred distinctions between the two, as musicologist Alan Lomax notes:

For more than two hundred years these two contrasting musical cultures dwelt side by side in America in a state of continually stimulating exchange and competition. Song material passed back and forth across the racial line so that it becomes increasingly difficult to say which group has contributed most to a song.

Alan Lomax, *The Folk Songs of North America*. Garden City, NY: Doubleday, 1960, p. xx.

---

some white singers were beginning to use black vocal techniques such as blue notes and sliding tones. Meanwhile, songs like "Blue-Tail Fly" may have originally belonged to one community or the other, but were adopted and enjoyed by both.

This process of cross-pollination continued to increase as workers of both races moved around the country to find work in timber, in coal mining, or in the industrialized North. Music writer Bill Flanagan notes that the influences of one group on the other, while clear, often went unacknowledged: "The two traditions crossed over and influenced one another all the time, though they were formally as separate as the front gate and the back door. One reason black and white [musicians] didn't always acknowledge how much they lifted from each other is that black and white men often resist admitting how much they have in common."[19]

As black and white styles—the most prevalent forms of folk music in America—developed and influenced each other, other branches of folk music were also stirring. In particular, ethnic groups who were newly immigrating to America brought their own music with them. Once in America, these immigrants formed vibrant communities that helped preserve and celebrate their music.

Chapter Three

New and Different Voices

More than any other nation, America has had the fertile soil from which the seeds of "people music" could grow in abundance.
—music historian Samuel L. Forcucci, *A Folk Song History of America*

America has always prided itself on being a nation of immigrants. From colonial days onward, the country has absorbed millions of people from a wide variety of cultures, ethnic backgrounds, and nationalities. These groups brought their own distinctive musical styles with them, and the result has made American folk music an ever-richer stew.

Folklorists recognize that this variety is crucial to a healthy and vibrant culture. They point out that it would be a dull world indeed if everyone had the same musical heritage and taste. Sarah Gertrude Knott, founder of the National Folk Festival, remarked about this issue in 1934: "Our national culture is being woven from the warp and woof of the variegated and colorful strains of many nations. No one would want to dull the richness of the pattern. How bleak indeed would be the cultural outlook for the future if we overlooked the distinctive, individual cultures in a universalized, standardized, regimented culture."[20]

The Cajuns

Musically speaking, one of the most interesting groups in America are the Cajuns. Cajuns are descendants of French families who, in the 1600s, settled along Canada's eastern seaboard. (Their name is a corruption of "Acadian," the French name for them.)

The Acadians were forced to leave Canada in the mid-1700s after refusing to join the British military in fighting French colonists. Many fled to the American colonies, particularly the swamps and bayous of Louisiana. Isolated from the world at large, they became tight-knit groups of hunters, trappers, and farmers who spoke their own version of French, created their own fiery cooking, and developed their own robust music.

Cajun music is a standout even in Louisiana, which, with its blend of French, Spanish, black, Caribbean, and Native American cultures, has always had an especially strong musical heritage. Music scholar Ann Allen Savoy asserts, "Few American states can claim a culture as varied, vibrant, and distinctive as Louisiana's . . . and [Cajun music is] among the state's greatest contributions."[21]

Cajun Music

Cajun music is based on traditional French folk dance music. However, over time (and despite the Cajuns' isolation in Louisiana) it mingled with the music of African Americans and Creoles (people of mixed French-Spanish-African-Caribbean descent). The result, by the early twentieth century, was an altogether spicier style, ancient French dance forms such as waltzes and quadrilles freely mixing with syncopated rhythms (rhythms that are off-center of the primary beat) and uninhibited singing.

It was still dance music, however, played by small groups at house dances. (In Cajun French, such a dance was called a *fais do-do*.) The groups typically featured an accordionist and/or one or two fiddle players, sometimes accompanied

Musicians gather to play Cajun music at a jam session in Louisiana.

by a triangle or other simple percussion. Vocalists often joined in as well.

The accordions used by Cajuns were button accordions, which could only play in one key (unlike modern accordions). Introduced by German American settlers, accordions were favorites with Cajuns because of their sturdy construction and volume. They could be heard in even the noisiest dance halls.

A number of important Cajun musicians emerged in the early decades of the twentieth century. One was fiddler Dennis McGee. In a biracial pairing unusual for the time, McGee often performed with Amédé Ardoin, a black Creole accordionist. Also outstanding was the husband-wife team of Joe and Cleoma Falcon. Cleoma Falcon was doubly unusual: She played guitar, not a common instrument among Cajuns then, and she was a female in a mostly male performing environment.

Música Tejana

West of Louisiana, meanwhile, another distinctive style was developing. Along the Texas-Mexico border, Tejanos—descendants of Spanish Mexican colonists—were, like the Cajuns, both preserving their traditional music and creating vibrant new styles. Music historian Manuel Peña writes, "Historically, Texas-Mexicans . . . are among the most musically productive regional groups in the Americas, having created several influential styles." [22]

Collectively these styles are called *música tejana*, translated informally as "Tex-Mex music." It developed in several different ways. Large dance ensembles, usually including trumpets, saxophones, and violins, were called *orquestas tejanas* or *orquestas típicas*. These played a variation on older styles of European dance music. Another well-known Tex-Mex format was a small group called a *conjunto* (band); it played a style called *norteño* (northern) that, like so many other folk styles, was working-class dance music.

While retaining many older and more traditional elements, *norteño* was also strongly influenced in the late 1800s by the large German immigrant population in central Texas. Many dance styles were borrowed from the German repertoire, such as polkas and schottisches. German music also influenced the *conjunto*'s instrumentation: In addition to guitar and *bajo sexto* (a large twelve-string guitar), a typical *conjunto* included as its lead instrument a German-style button accordion.

Corridos

Another classic form of Texas-Mexican folk music is the *corrido*, a type of ballad descended, in part, from Spanish ballads of the Middle Ages. Typically, *corridos* use four-line stanzas and simple tunes in fast waltz or polka rhythms. Typical *corridos* narrated stories about notable incidents, such as barroom shoot-outs or natural disasters, or gave highly politicized renditions of events such as peasants' battles against injustice.

Corridos were often performed by wandering *guitarreros* (guitarist-singers) or by migrant workers as they

A conjunto group plays working class folk music called norteño *featuring its trademark accordion.*

traveled the countryside. The songs' simple melodies and short ranges— usually less than an octave—made them easy to sing loudly by even the most modest voice; scholar Américo Paredes points out that the *corrido* was designed to be performed "at the top of the singer's voice, an essential part of the *corrido* style."[23]

By the early decades of the twentieth century many notable musicians had emerged from the Texas-Mexican border region. Standouts included accor-dion virtuoso Narciso Martinez and legendary guitarist-singer Lydia Mendoza, known as "the songstress of the poor" for her championing of the oppressed.

Sailors and Other Workers

Ethnic groups like the Cajuns and Texas Mexicans were not the only ones responsible for the distinctive styles of folk music developing in America. Sometimes laborers thrown together by their shared work developed distinctive songs all their own.

Railroad workers and lumberjacks were two such groups. "Casey Jones" and "I've Been Working on the Railroad" were typical railroading songs, while "Once More A-Lumberin' Go" and "The Jam on Jerry's Rocks" came from the lumberjack repertoire. (In this case, "jam" referred to a logjam.)

Many American sailor songs were adaptations of British sea chanteys;

Narciso Martinez is an accordion virtuoso from the Texas-Mexican border region.

others were influenced by cultures outside of the British Isles. Oceangoing vessels, such as whaling ships, routinely traveled the world; sailors were thus apt to pick up musical influences from all over, while crew members picked up in faraway ports contributed further influences. As a result, for example, some American sailing songs are in minor keys, reflecting a Mediterranean and/or Jewish touch.

Not all sailor songs were for work times; sometimes they were simply for enjoyment. These "fo'c'sle songs" (so called because they were sung in or around a ship's living quarters, or forecastle) helped counteract the boredom of long hours and turn thoughts to home and loved ones. A typical fo'c'sle song was the ballad "Leave Her, Johnny." (In this case, the "her" referred to the ship—the song was ceremonially sung at the end of a voyage.)

Cowboy Songs

The cowboys of the Old West were, perhaps, the most famous of all song-producing work groups in America. The main period of the Old West lasted only a brief time, roughly from 1865 to 1890, and cowboys were a relatively small part of the population. Nonetheless, cowboys had a potent impact on American society, becoming powerfully mythic figures and symbols of freedom, ruggedness, and independence. The impact of cowboys on American folk music was equally important.

They were an ethnically diverse group. There were English and Irish

"Like a Nuclear Bomb"

Many musicians with strong ties to their ethnic roots have found treasures in their own cultures. Cajun accordionist Marc Savoy is one such performer. He comments,

[When] I grew up, I never rebelled against what my parents [were doing]. Especially when I started school, when I saw what my peers were pursuing. Actually, I tried as a young kid to get into football and sports, but I thought that it was so mundane and trivial compared to what my grandparents or my parents were doing. My mother used to tell me, "Why do you want to pursue what all these old people [are doing]? You know, learn their stories, learn their music, learn how to speak French—why do you want to do that?" "Mom," I said, "this stuff is so fantastic. It's just a matter of time when the rest of the world finds out about this; this is gonna explode like a nuclear bomb."

Quoted in Robert Santelli, Holly George-Warren, and Jim Brown, eds., *American Roots Music*. New York: Abrams, 2001, p. 124.

cowboys, Hispanic cowboys, African American cowboys, German cowboys, even a handful of Jewish cowboys. These diverse backgrounds provided ample source material for the cowboys' large and durable collection of songs. New melodies were sometimes created from scratch, but often cowboys simply put new lyrics to existing melodies.

Cowboys routinely spent months at a time on the prairies, performing backbreaking work in almost complete isolation. Composing and performing songs, usually on easy-to-carry instruments like harmonicas and fiddles, were good ways to pass the time. Like all true folk songs, cowboy songs were anonymously written. Folklorist John A. Lomax, who studied them extensively, wrote, "In only a few instances have I been able to discover the authorship of any [cowboy] songs. They seem to have sprung up quietly and mysteriously as does the grass on the plains."[24]

Singing to the Cattle

Cowboys sang for many of the usual reasons, especially to pass the time during the long hours on the job or while sitting around a nighttime fire (if on the trail) or in the bunkhouse (if on the ranch). However, one unusual situation was a frequent cause of cowboy song:

Many of their performances were for audiences of cattle.

Cowboys on cattle drives were responsible for keeping hundreds of easily spooked animals calm. Those who had night shifts discovered that soft singing helped settle the animals and lessened the chances of a stampede. (It also helped keep singers from falling asleep late at night.) Singing on the trail became so important that a cowhand frequently stood a better chance of being hired if he had a good singing voice.

There are many examples of common cowboy songs. One is "I Ride an Old Paint" ("Paint" was a common

Cowboys sing around a campfire. On long cattle drives singing passed the time and also helped to calm the cattle.

"Hard to Improve Upon"

Musicologist Alan Lomax had this to say about the ways in which folk songs were adapted to changing times:

Most of our frontier ballads were composed by [an] anonymous . . . poet [who] was steeped in the song lore of his region, and was passionately identified with the group for whom he sang. In composing a new ballad, he took a well-known traditional song that told as nearly as possible the story he wished to tell, and altered only as far as his theme demanded. In the opening stanzas he gave [it a] fresh topical setting and for the rest confined himself to changing names or adding new lines here or there. Even these new lines generally came from the traditional stock. Thus some of our ballads set out from Britain, served their time on deep water, lived in lumberjack bunk-houses, rode the western range and now fly with the jet pilots. The folk poet is a conservative, building solidly out of his tradition, for both he and his audience find the old songs hard to improve upon.

Alan Lomax, *The Folk Songs of North America*. Garden City, NY: Doubleday, 1960, pp. xxvii–xxviii.

name for a horse). Another is an enormous epic, "The Old Chisholm Trail," which had hundreds of verses made up by anonymous singers over the years.

Because of its long and disjointed creation, the verses of "The Old Chisholm Trail" have no narrative continuity. However, cowboy songs were usually more straightforward ballads; an example is "Jesse James," about the famous train robber. Overall, the topics generally concerned daily cowboy life and its pleasures, pains, dangers, and rewards. Forcucci notes, "In the ballad form he [a singer] was able to tell about cowboys who led dangerous lives fighting off Indians, outlaws, wild animals, and dust storms; he could talk about big drives and the danger from stampedes; he could even talk about that great range in the sky, which was his way of describing heaven." [25]

Many Styles

As groups like cowboys, Tejanos, and Cajuns developed and preserved their music, other groups were also doing the same. In particular, new groups of immigrants arrived in America in massive waves during the decades around the turn of the twentieth century. Some of these new arrivals were from Asia,

Jazz musicians play klezmer music, a style of music brought to America by Jewish immigrants.

gary, Romania, France, and Germany. Each group brought its own music: The Poles and Germans had their accordion-driven dance tunes; the Italians had their sweet, sad mandolin songs; and the Jews (roughly 10 percent of all Eastern European and Russian immigrants) had their vibrant klezmer music.

This influx of new people would soon have a dramatic impact on American folk music. At first the immigrants, like new arrivals before them, remained relatively separate from each other, divided by ethnic, language, and social barriers. As a result, the musical styles stayed separate as well.

However, the compartmentalization of American folk music was breaking down. At first this was due to improved transportation. Better roads connected formerly isolated regions, and railroads made steady inroads into the western frontier. Musicians could travel with increasing ease from region to region, and, inevitably, they began to influence each other.

Soon another factor was also at play. Improved technology in the form of radio and phonograph records had a profound and explosive effect on American folk music. They helped destroy barriers separating isolated pockets of ethnic or national groupings and ushered in the next major phase in folk music's history.

but most—an estimated 20.5 million between 1871 and 1911 alone—were European or Russian.

In one of the most dramatic population shifts in history, these immigrants came in waves from places like Italy, Poland, Czechoslovakia, Hun-

Chapter Four

Folk Goes National

It must have seemed like a miracle to dial this magic box, get some wild Appalachian recording, and then turn the dial a little bit more and get . . . big-band music, gospel, blues, and the Grand Ole Opry.
—singer Bonnie Raitt on the advent of radio, quoted in *American Roots Music*

Better transportation was the first force of change to be felt. As roads and railroads improved, professional musicians moved more frequently between urban and rural areas. Typically, these musicians belonged to traveling productions such as medicine shows and chautauquas (tent shows that combined education and entertainment).

One such traveling performance was the minstrel show. In these revues white musicians, dressed in "blackface" (caricatures of black people), joked and sang in a parody of African American style. The shows provided white northern audiences with a hu-

morous (if false) view of supposedly carefree plantation life.

Minstrel Shows

Minstrel shows seem grotesquely racist from a modern standpoint, but they were an important part of America's musical history. They were early instances of folk music crossing racial and social barriers, introducing elements of black culture (however distorted) to white audiences. Writer Kip Lornell notes, "Minstrel shows represent the country's first major exploitation and presentation of folk culture to a mainstream audience."[26]

Some songs associated with minstrel shows, such as "Blue-Tail Fly," originated in the black community. However, many were versions of familiar white folk-dance melodies like "Turkey in the Straw." Also perennial favorites were folk song–like compositions by professional songwriters; the best of these writers was the gifted Stephen Foster, whose many compositions include

Accomplished songwriters like Stephen Foster (left) wrote songs that crossed color boundaries while folk musicians like Cajun fiddler Dennis McGee (right) remained popular only within their communities.

"Camptown Races" and "My Old Kentucky Home."

The line between minstrel songs and genuine folk music was often blurred. This was because the general public— black and white alike—routinely adopted songs like Foster's so wholeheartedly that the music quickly became part of folk culture. Epstein writes, "As no one knows how much of the early minstrel music [derived] from folk music, and many minstrel songs later entered the folk repertory and were transmitted orally, disentangling one from the other is a herculean task."[27]

Records

Minstrel shows continued into the early years of the twentieth century, although their popularity waned. Meanwhile, a new technology was transforming the way people listened to music. Though crude by modern standards, early phonograph records were a revolutionary development; since windup players did not require electricity, even isolated farm families could thrill to hearing music recorded far away.

For musicians this development was revolutionary. Records essentially erased geographic and stylistic barriers. A fiddler from Kentucky could listen to a trumpeter from New Orleans, while a blues singer in Mississippi could pick up the latest pop tune from New York.

The earliest recordings were too poor to record some music well, but by the 1920s the technology was much improved. Ensembles such as string bands could be heard with reasonable clarity. As a result, a number of companies began offering recordings in a variety of folk styles.

The First Recorded Hillbilly Music

Early commercial folk recordings were of traditional white music. The first may have been Texas fiddler Eck Robertson's "Sallie Goodin" in 1922. The next year a talent scout for Okeh Records, Ralph Peer, recorded Fiddlin'

A minstrel group comprised of white musicians wearing black makeup performs in 1925.

John Carson, who had a strong following around Atlanta, Georgia.

Carson's recording, "Little Old Log Cabin in the Lane," sold well even beyond the Atlanta area. Encouraged, Peer began making regular tours of the South and found a number of popular performers. Sales were good, and other companies followed Peer's example. Exact figures do not exist, but it has been estimated that 65 million traditional white folk recordings were sold between 1925 and 1932.

At first no one knew exactly what to call the music. It was variously referred to as "old-time southern tunes," "hill country music," or simply "old-time music." But when Peer gave one of his groups the name "Hill Billies," this term (as one word) became a catchall for all rural white music. Hill-billy music was born.

"Race Records"
Meanwhile, record sales for other kinds of popular music were also booming. Recordings by musicians such as *norteño* singer Mendoza and Cajun fiddler McGee were popular, although almost exclusively within their respective communities. More exotic sounds, from Hawaiian "slack-key" (slide) guitars to Eastern European polkas, also found small but enthusiastic audiences.

By far the biggest sellers were "race records"—a term that lumped together all recordings aimed at African Americans, including blues, spirituals, and spoken sermons. Blues records were the big sellers; the first big blues hit, singer Mamie Smith's 1920 "Crazy Blues," eventually sold 2 million copies.

Blues continued to have robust sales, and by 1927 roughly ten blues records were being released every week. These were promoted heavily in the black community, Filene notes: "They were sold in record shops, mail-order catalogs, saloons, book stores, barber shops, drug stores, furniture stores, and cigar stands, and they quickly became important elements in African American community life." [28]

Radio
During this period another technological marvel was storming the country. In 1920 radio station KDKA in Pittsburgh made the first commercial broadcast. Radio was a sensation, and by 1923 most major American cities boasted their own stations.

In its early days radio seemed miraculous. Since airwaves were uncluttered and stations largely unregulated, listeners could sometimes pick up signals from hundreds of miles away. Some "border radio" stations, broadcasting from Mexico, were so powerful that they blanketed much of North America.

The magical new technology thus helped stitch the nation, and its musical heritage, together. Even people in remote rural areas could hear far-off musicians performing live. Singer Bonnie Raitt notes, "Radio provided the crucial link between the musicians and the music in one farmland, mountain, swamp, or urban community and countless others." [29]

Blues guitarist Muddy Waters (left) was profoundly influenced by the music he heard Sonny Boy Williamson II (right) play during the 1940s.

The *Opry* and the Blues

Folk music was integral to radio from the beginning. Many stations featured regular live folk performances, especially hillbilly music. Most of these shows were popular only regionally, but some acquired national reputations—like the famous *Grand Ole Opry* on WSM in Nashville, Tennessee.

Debuting in 1925, this long-running weekly show, known for its down-home flavor, soon had a loyal following far beyond the South; by 1948 one survey estimated that the *Opry* was being heard in 10 million homes every week. Among the countless stars it launched were Uncle Dave Macon, Ernest Tubb, Minnie Pearl, Hank Williams, and the program's longtime host, Roy Acuff.

Blues shows were also heard, although they were not regularly scheduled until the 1940s. The most famous was *King Biscuit Time* on station KFFA in Helena, Arkansas; named for its sponsor, King Biscuit Flour, this daily show featured two virtuoso performers—harmonica player Sonny Boy Williamson II and guitarist Robert Junior Lockwood. *King Biscuit Time*, heard throughout the Arkansas-Mississippi Delta, profoundly influenced an emerging generation of blues musicians, including B.B. King and Muddy Waters, who listened to it while resting from their work on the region's plantations and farms.

The Impact of the *Opry*

The Grand Ole Opry *radio show was terrifically influential on those who fell under its spell in its early days. Writer Robert Santelli comments:*

The influence . . . of the *Grand Ole Opry* radio show is astounding. Each Saturday night throughout the South and beyond, particularly in the Twenties, Thirties, and Forties, thousands of households—white and black—listened intently to the program. Musicians counted on learning new songs and picking up ideas from the *Opry* performers. The number of would-be musicians who were inspired to pick up the guitar or banjo or muster the courage to sing because of what they heard on the radio is impossible to calculate, but the total must be huge.

Robert Santelli, "Introduction," in *American Roots Music*, eds. Robert Santelli, Holly George-Warren, and Jim Brown. New York: Abrams, 2001, p. 13.

The Carters

As radio expanded folk's popularity and reach, the music began to change. For one thing, the term "hillbilly" was dropped in favor of "country," which included the smoother, more pop-oriented music often featured on shows like the *Opry*. Also, folk musicians for the first time attained genuine national stature thanks to the exposure they got from records and radio.

One such group was the Carter Family: Sara (autoharp and lead vocals), her husband A.P. (bass vocals), and Sara's cousin Maybelle (guitar and vocals). Raised in Virginia's Clinch Valley, the Carters were steeped in well-known old-time songs, and A.P. was also a shrewd collector of more obscure tunes.

Their records sold phenomenally well, and many of the songs they introduced became familiar standards, including "Wildwood Flower," "The Wabash Cannonball," and "Will the Circle Be Unbroken?" Maybelle's guitar playing was also influential; the "Carter lick"—melody played on the lower strings, chords strummed on the higher strings—became a basic technique for generations of guitarists. Music writers Dean Tudor and Nancy Tudor note, "*Everyone* in country music has [had] at least one Carter song in his/her repertoire." [30]

The Singing Brakeman

Another standout of the era was Jimmie Rodgers. His first recordings were made at the same time and place as the Carters: June 1927 in an old hat factory in Bristol, a town on the Virginia-Tennessee border. The recordist was Peer, the pioneering record scout who had coined the term "hillbilly."

Born in Meridian, Mississippi, in the heart of blues country, Rodgers was deeply influenced by African American folk music. He briefly worked for the railroad, but after contracting tuberculosis he was unable to handle strenuous

The Carter Family's songs remain widely regarded and influential staples of country music.

physical labor and tried his hand at playing music professionally. Within a few years of his 1927 debut, Rodgers was a national star.

The Singing Brakeman, as he was nicknamed for his former occupation, was a gifted songwriter and a warm, inviting vocalist—especially when he let loose with his infectious yodel. Among Rodgers's many hits were "T for Texas," "In the Jailhouse Now," and "Blue Yodel #9." The latter, from 1930, was an early example of a biracial recording session; the legendary jazz trumpeter Louis Armstrong accompanied Rodgers.

Preserving the Music

Entrepreneurs were behind the booming sales of records by artists like Rodgers and the Carters. However, not everyone who recorded folk music had profit in mind. In particular, a small group of folklorists—scholars and serious collectors—sought to preserve the music for the future.

An important figure in this field was John A. Lomax, who had collected cowboy songs while growing up on a Texas ranch in the late 1800s and continued his studies as a graduate student at Harvard University. Lomax's 1910 book *Cowboy Songs and Other Frontier Ballads* featured an introduction by former president Theodore Roosevelt, who deeply loved the West; Roosevelt's enthusiastic endorsement helped popularize the book.

Another example was a 1927 publication, *American Songbag*, a collection of traditional tunes edited by the famous poet Carl Sandburg. In addition, a number of amateur folklorists made important contributions of their own. One was Charles Lummis, a colorful California journalist and civil rights activist who preserved, early in the twentieth century, almost four hundred Spanish-language songs on fragile wax cylinders.

Government Sponsorship

During this period the federal government began to officially recognize folk music as an important cultural heritage. As a result, it began contributing significantly to folk song preservation. In 1928, for example, the Library of Congress created the Archive of American Folk Song, a repository for recordings.

During the Great Depression of the 1930s, funding for folklorists continued. For example, the Works Progress Administration, an agency that created jobs for the unemployed, sponsored several folk-related projects. These recorded songs in a variety of settings, including such "urban folk" as garment workers in New York City, steelworkers in Pennsylvania, and railroad workers in Chicago.

President Franklin D. Roosevelt and First Lady Eleanor Roosevelt helped focus national attention in other ways as well. FDR stated that his favorite song was "Home on the Range." When Eleanor Roosevelt attended Virginia's White Top folk festival in 1933, the accompanying publicity caused attendance to soar from a previous average

The Great Popularizers

John and Alan Lomax had an enormous impact on the course of folk music, thanks to their efforts to popularize it. Historian Benjamin Filene comments:

The Lomaxes were the first . . . to promote a coherent vision of America's folk music heritage. To promote their canon they relied not on a popular interpreter of folk songs but on exemplars [models] from the folk culture itself. They enlisted the full array of mass media—newspapers, radio, movie newsreels, concerts, and records—to transform rural folk musicians into celebrities. In effect they spread their vision of American music by integrating folk into mass culture.

Benjamin Filene, *Romancing the Folk: Public Memory and American Roots Music*. Chapel Hill: University of North Carolina Press, 2000, p. 57.

Alan Lomax (left) documents songs and record albums in an effort to preserve America's folk music tradition.

---

of four thousand to almost twenty thousand. The Roosevelts also sponsored nine multi-racial concerts of folk music and dance at the White House.

The Lomax Recordings

In the 1930s Lomax and his then teenage son, Alan, created a massive, landmark folk song preservation project. Sponsored by the Library of Congress, they crisscrossed the country with a "portable" recording machine (a five-hundred-pound unit built into their car). In order to find "pure" performers relatively untouched by current pop music, they sought out the most isolated communities possible, such as plantations, ranches, lumber camps, and prisons.

Among the most fruitful locales were southern prison farms, where they talked wardens into letting them record African American inmates singing field hollers, blues, and gospel. These songs became some of the most powerful of the thousands the Lomaxes preserved. Alan Lomax later recalled, "The prisoners in those penitentiaries simply had dynamite in their performances."[31]

The Lomax recordings were so extensive and varied that they essentially formed a portrait in song of America. Archibald MacLeish, a distinguished poet and Librarian of Congress, declared that they were "a body

Folklorist Alan Lomax plays guitar in 1946.

of words and music which tells more about the American people than all the miles of their quadruple-lane expressways and all the acres of their billboard-plastered cities."[32]

"Folk Music in Overdrive"

Despite the efforts of folklorists like the Lomaxes to preserve "pure" folk, the music was increasingly influenced by commercial considerations. For example, old-time string music evolved by the 1940s into a sophisticated, streamlined style called bluegrass. (The name was a nod to the nickname of Kentucky, the Blue Grass State.)

Within bluegrass, one name stood out. Mandolin player Bill Monroe dominated the genre so completely that he is generally considered its founder. Monroe's band, the Bluegrass Boys, expanded the classic fiddle-banjo lineup to include mandolin, guitar, and string bass, providing much stronger rhythmic and sonic variety. Monroe also fixed the classic bluegrass repertoire, which mixed newly composed songs with old ballads and religious songs.

Bluegrass stressed lightning-fast solos, complex harmonies, and a plaintive vocal style known as "high lonesome." The overall effect was of speed, smoothness, and a bittersweet mixture of joy and sorrow. Alan Lomax called it "folk music in overdrive with a silvery, rippling, pining sound."[33]

Blues Changes

As bluegrass evolved, so did the blues. In the 1940s, as part of a longstanding

Mandolin player Bill Monroe (left, pictured with his brother Charlie) is considered the founder of bluegrass music.

trend, huge numbers of African Americans left the South in search of better lives in the industrialized North. In particular, some Mississippi blues musicians migrated to Chicago, Illinois.

There they began to experiment with adding drums to their bands and amplifying their instruments; electric instruments were at that time a new and exciting development. These changes gave the blues a powerful new edge.

Once an acoustic, languid style, it took on a driving urban energy.

Urban blues, as exemplified by the Chicago scene, had a varied repertoire. Sometimes it used updated versions of country blues tunes; sometimes it used new songs. Some lyrics gloried in the pleasures of the city; others expressed nostalgia for the rural life the musicians and their listeners had abandoned. Filene writes that urban blues musicians "treated their downhome past as a resource to be drawn on, a memory that they could share with their audiences." [34]

Guitarist Muddy Waters (left) and pianist Otis Spann (right) were prominent blues musicians in Chicago during the 1940s.

Pianist Otis Spann and bassist-songwriter Willie Dixon were two prominent musicians on the Chicago scene, but the undisputed king was singer-guitarist McKinley Morganfield, better known as Muddy Waters. This former tractor driver from Mississippi crystallized the link between traditional country music and the exciting new music of the city. Singer-guitarist Keb' Mo' asserts, "Muddy Waters [was] the consummate connection between the Delta and Chicago." [35]

More Evolution

Other folk-based musicians were also evolving during this period. For example, in Louisiana the Hackberry Ramblers pioneered changes in Cajun music. The band probably was the first to add country songs (in French) to its repertoire, to drop the accordion as a primary instrument, and to electrify (the musicians hooked up to a parked Model T).

Farther west in the dancehalls of Oklahoma and Texas, a new folk-influenced style was developing. Western swing incorporated an eccentric group of instruments, including saxophones, accordions, pedal steel guitars, and fiddles. It also borrowed from everywhere, blending country and cowboy songs with jazz, blues, polkas, Hawaiian, *norteño*, and more. Spade Cooley and Milton Brown helped pioneer this infectious style, but the king of western swing was Bob Wills, whose many hits included "San Antonio Rose" and "Careless Love."

Bob Wills (left) conducts his western swing band in the 1940s.

Western swing, electric blues, and other styles had blossomed thanks to improved transportation and technology. The changes had also affected traditional folk, and the audiences for every style were growing. Nonetheless, the general public was not particularly aware of folk as a national trea-sure. Music historian Robert Cantwell notes that for many people a folk song was "a thing found mostly in books, whether it was a scholarly collection, a school text used for singing, or a campfire songbook."[36] Fortunately, the seeds had been planted for a major folk boom.

Chapter Five

The Folk Revival Begins

You can have your Radio City Music Hall . . . and your tuxedoes, but as far as I'm concerned the best music I ever heard came out of [an] old shack in Townley, Alabama.

—Pete Seeger, quoted in Cantwell, *When We Were Good*

This folk boom began in the mid-1940s, a major revival during which interest in the music soared to unprecedented heights. The boom began as a regional phenomenon. However, America was now firmly connected, musically speaking, by radio, records, and speedy travel (not to mention the new technology of television); the increase in folkies—folk song enthusiasts—was thus primarily a national phenomenon.

The folk revival was roughly split in two parts, more or less corresponding to a generational shift. Both periods shared important similarities: They closely linked folk music with politics and social change, and they connected the music with a desire to return to simpler times. The folk boom, occurring alongside and commenting on some of the most wrenching political changes in American history, was, in the words of Jabbour, "one of the most striking features of Twentieth-Century America."[37]

Politics and Music

The connection between folk music and politics had existed in various forms for centuries prior to the 1940s. Its roots can be seen in the broadsides popular in colonial times. These song parodies had provided satiric commentaries on current events and issues.

In later decades folk music—the "music of the people"—was closely associated in many instances with political or social causes. For example, in the early and mid-1800s, abolitionists (activists who opposed slavery) frequently adapted folk tunes. They gave these familiar melodies new words that supported their sentiments.

By the 1930s folk music was closely associated with reform social movements. For example, a number of groups, including labor organizations and the Communist and Socialist parties, used songs to address the social problems of the Great Depression. Sometimes these songs were old tunes refitted with new words, and sometimes they were newly written, as in "Joe Hill," a song by Alfred Hayes and Earl Robinson about an executed labor hero.

The connection between social movements and folk music persisted into the 1940s and World War II. It continued as well into the postwar era, the time of recovery from the war's end in 1945 into the 1950s.

During this period the world seemed increasingly unsafe in many ways. Worries about the atomic bomb, tension between democratic and Communist countries, and mounting civil rights struggles made many people yearn for

Influential folk musician Pete Seeger plays the banjo in 1955. Seeger connected social issues with music and wrote numerous songs that remain beloved folk standards.

a return to simpler times. Folk music, with its emphasis on simple instruments and songs of rural life, as well as its heritage of speaking out on social issues, held an obvious appeal, especially for those concerned with the plight of working-class and poor people.

Pete Seeger

During this period, one of the central figures connecting folk music with liberal social causes was a lanky, energetic banjo player and singer named Pete Seeger. Born into a distinguished musical family in New York State, Seeger fell in love with folk music while attending Harvard University in the 1930s. He later recalled that folk's down-to-earth qualities appealed to both his musical taste and his passion for social justice:

> I discovered there was some good music in my country which I never heard on the radio. . . . I liked the strident vocal tones of the singers, the vigorous dancing. The words of the songs had all the meat of life on them. Their humor had a bite, it was not trivial. Their tragedy was real, not sentimental. In comparison, most of the pop music of the thirties seemed to me weak and soft, with its endless variations on "Baby, baby I need you." [38]

Seeger dropped out of Harvard to work at the Library of Congress, cataloging and transcribing songs. Settling in New York City's Greenwich Village, he quickly joined the city's small but growing folk music scene. He took active roles in a variety of projects that mixed music and politics.

One such project was a short-lived but influential performing group, the Almanac Singers. The Almanacs, which had shifting personnel, specialized in blues and hillbilly tunes, old-time music, hymns, and political songs. They sang at events such as liberal fund-raisers and made two albums; the first urged pacifism, the second was a collection of labor songs. Several members of the Almanacs, including Seeger, remained influential in the folk music world, although the group disbanded after barely two years.

"The Tuning Fork of America"

Another organization Seeger founded was People's Songs, which promoted the distribution of both traditional folk tunes and topical songs. At its peak, People's Songs had several branches around the country, maintained a library of songs, published songbooks and a monthly bulletin, and sponsored summer camps for kids and concert tours. The *New York Times* noted in 1946: "People's Songs keeps a musical stethoscope on the heartbeat of the nation, translating current events into notes and lyrics." [39]

In addition to his connection with these groups, Seeger was a composer. A number of the songs he wrote or cowrote, including "If I Had a Hammer," "Turn, Turn, Turn," and "Where Have All the Flowers Gone," have become familiar folk standards. Further-

The Golden Years

The golden years of the folk music revival saw a peak both in widely popular commercial folk and in the music's less popular but more authentic strains. Ronald D. Cohen comments:

Folk music—acoustic, traditional, with or without a message, hard to pin down but seemingly identifiable; blues, Cajun, klezmer, old-time, country, Celtic, bluegrass—would continue to flow along in both commercial and private channels, as it had long done, continuing to capture and charm. If folk reached its commercial peak sometime in the mid-1960s, this was only a fleeting recognition of its potential ability to reach out beyond the small, scattered groups of performers and political activists who had long been its champions. The story neither begins in 1940 nor ends in 1970; but this was a period when a remarkable number of performers, collectors, organizers, managers, academics, journalists, record company owners, writers, store owners, and many others coalesced to promote the music.

Ronald D. Cohen, *Rainbow Quest: The Folk Music Revival and American Society, 1940–70.* Amherst, MA: University of Massachusetts Press, 2002, p. 289.

more, he tirelessly recorded and performed, with others and as a solo singer.

Seeger's sturdy voice, robust stage presence, and passion for group singing made him one of the most recognizable figures in the folk scene; countless listeners—especially young people—were inspired to take up folk music after hearing a Seeger concert. Overall, Seeger had an enormous impact on the direction of folk music during the postwar years and for decades to come. Writer and radio host Studs Terkel, acknowledging Seeger's iconic status, once called him "the tuning fork of America." [40]

The Weavers

In 1948 Seeger cofounded a quartet, the Weavers, with singer-guitarist Fred Hellerman and singers Ronnie Gilbert and Lee Hays. This group did more than any other in its day to bring folk music to widespread, mainstream audiences. (It was not an immediate success, however; a radio contest to name the group yielded such results as "The Off-Keys" and "The Undertakers." Not surprisingly, the singers chose a name that reflected their interest in weaving together folk styles.)

The Weavers were eager to find a wider audience beyond the relatively

Pete Seeger (left) rehearses with his band the Weavers before a show in 1952.

small group of folkies who followed them already. Seeger commented that they hoped to "make a dent in the wall that seemed to be between us and the American people."[41] The group therefore focused on glossy productions with lush harmonies and orchestrations. (In some cases, they cleaned up lyrics as well; their rendition of "Good Night Irene," for instance, eliminated a verse about morphine and changed the line "I'll get you in my dreams" to "I'll see you in my dreams.")

The Weavers' polished version of folk music appealed strongly to the record-buying public, and they became a huge success. Their many hits included both traditional folk tunes (like "On Top of Old Smokey") and newly written songs (such as "So Long, It's Been Good to Know Yuh".) Their version of "Good Night Irene" was a number-one hit in 1950; it was so widely known that it even inspired a parody, "Please Say Goodnight to the Guy, Irene (So I Can Get Some Sleep)."

Lead Belly

The composer of "Good Night Irene" was, like Seeger, an iconic figure in folk music: an African American singer and guitarist named Huddie Ledbetter, better known as Lead Belly. Lead Belly contributed to folk in a number of important ways, including his influential performing style. He played mostly a twelve-string guitar, which gave the music a distinctive jangly sound, and—though his voice was not beautiful—he sang with tremendous passion, understanding, and rhythmic sense.

Perhaps even more important, however, were the many songs of his own composition or drawn from the vast repertoire of black folk music that he introduced to the American public. A number of these became familiar standards, including "The Midnight Special," "Rock Island Line," and, of course, "Good Night Irene." Songwriter Earl Robinson comments that few people "would dispute that Lead Belly was America's greatest and most creative folk singer."[42]

As a young man in rural Louisiana, Lead Belly sang and played guitar and accordion for local dances and parties. He was known for having an unusually wide repertoire. He could sing everything, it seemed, from blues, field hollers, and spirituals to pop, cowboy songs, children's tunes, and traditional ballads.

But Lead Belly also had a violent temper, and by the 1930s he was serving time for attempted homicide in a Louisiana prison farm. John and Alan Lomax met him there and recorded him extensively for their Library of Congress project. The singer won parole in 1934 and settled in New York City.

He worked as the Lomax family chauffeur and began a successful performing career. New York's (mostly white) community of folk enthusiasts and leftist activists warmly welcomed the singer, although he was never especially politically active and rarely wrote political songs. (An exception was "Bourgeois Blues," which made a biting commentary on racism in Washington, D.C.)

Iconic folk singer Lead Belly strums his twelve-string guitar.

"This Land Is Your Land"

A third key figure during this period was a close friend of, and frequent collaborator with, both Seeger and Lead Belly. This was Woodrow Wilson Guthrie. Born in rural Oklahoma, Woody Guthrie had a rough and impoverished childhood and left home at fifteen. He eventually migrated west to California with thousands of other Oklahomans who had been made homeless by dust storms.

Singing and playing in the hobo and migrant camps that sprang up during the Great Depression, Guthrie experienced firsthand the poverty and misery that poor people routinely faced. It instilled in him a fierce sense of justice and a lasting sympathy for political causes. (Guthrie also had deep faith in the power of song to conquer evil; he painted a message on his battered guitar reading, "This machine kills fascists.")

Eventually settling in New York City, Guthrie became a member of the Almanac Singers. He recorded for both the Library of Congress and commercial record companies. Guthrie also wrote a classic autobiography, *Bound for Glory*, and was a frequent performer on his own or with colleagues like Seeger.

Politically minded Woody Guthrie plays his guitar, which according to him was a machine that could kill fascists.

"I Am Out to Fight Those Songs"

This is an excerpt from a statement by Woody Guthrie that was on a popular poster and still serves as a manifesto for many within the folk music movement.

I hate a song that makes you think that you are not any good. I hate a song that makes you think that you are just born to lose. Bound to lose. No good to nobody. No good for nothing. Because you are too old or too young or too fat or too slim. Too ugly or too this or too that. Songs that run you down or poke fun at you on account of your bad luck or hard traveling.

I am out to fight those songs to my very last breath of air and my last drop of blood. I am out to sing songs that will prove to you that this is your world and that if it has hit you pretty hard and knocked you for a dozen loops, no matter what color, what size you are, how you are built, I am out to sing the songs that make you take pride in yourself and in your work. And the songs that I sing are made up for the most part by all sorts of folks just about like you.

Woody Guthrie Website, "Woody Guthrie Poster Text." www.woody guthrie.org/woodyguthrie/shop/media/woodyguthrieposter.htm.

Guthrie's performing style and persona were markedly different from those of his friend. Seeger had arrived at liberal politics, pacifist philosophy, and folk music through his comfortable eastern upbringing and university education. Guthrie, meanwhile, was a poor man from the West who had led a colorful and often difficult life; this was reflected in his unpretentious demeanor and clothes, his earthy manner, and his no-frills guitar style.

It was also reflected in the plain-spoken words of his songs. Guthrie had a gift for vivid portraits of ordinary people and their struggles with homelessness, corruption, and injustice. Jabbour writes, "A compulsive writer with a keen eye and a sharp wit, he [composed] songs on contemporary issues, drawing on classic folk tunes and genres for his settings." [43]

By the time a hereditary neurological disease incapacitated him, Guthrie had written about a thousand songs. Some

*During the 1940s and 1950s Senator Joseph McCarthy fueled anti-Communist
sentiment throughout the United States.*

were about folk-hero outlaws—as in
"Pretty Boy Floyd," his ode to a famous
bank robber—while others praised
America's natural wonders, as did "Roll
On, Columbia," his ode to a mighty river.
Meanwhile, there was the most famous
Guthrie song of all, "This Land Is Your
Land"; originally a bitter commentary on
injustice, it eventually lost its political
verses and became a familiar part of the
American musical mainstream.

The Red Scare

Singers like Guthrie made no secret of
their liberal beliefs. Such beliefs,

however, could be hazardous. From the
late 1940s into the mid-1950s a conservative political movement affected
virtually every aspect of American
life—including folk singers—by trying
to equate liberal activism with anti-
American feelings.

During those years the so-called Cold
War posed the Communist Soviet
Union and the democratic United States
as enemies. The Red Scare, named for
the Soviet red flag, was a massive wave
of anti-Communist feeling that swept
America. Senator Joseph McCarthy of
Wisconsin and other politicians fueled

emotions by spearheading highly publicized investigations of people accused of anti-Americanism.

Many entertainers were blacklisted—denied work—as a result of these accusations and investigations. Countless careers and lives were ruined, or at least stunted. Among them were the Weavers, who were forced to disband as recording and concert opportunities dried up. Some, including Alan Lomax and singer Josh White, were forced to flee overseas. Singer and guitarist Dave Van Ronk, another key figure in the folk scene, bluntly states, "The Red Scare . . . damn near killed the folk revival in its tracks."[44]

The *Anthology*

The Red Scare faded away by the late 1950s, as it became clear that McCarthy and others had overstated the Communist threat within America. Fortunately for the folk music revival, interest did not die out completely in the meantime. In fact, a watershed event occurred in the midst of the Red Scare: the 1952 release of the *Anthology of American Folk Music*.

The *Anthology* was the brainchild of Harry Smith, a brilliant and eccentric musicologist. It consisted of eighty-four recordings from his massive private collection, released on six phonograph records by the small Folkways label. These recordings embraced a wide array of blues, ballads, old-time fiddling, spirituals, and more, mostly by performers mysterious and obscure even to hard-core folk enthusiasts.

All were recorded within a single five-year span, 1927–1935, and all had once been available for purchase. Smith was interested only in commercial records, not scholarly field recordings. As writer Greil Marcus notes, he "wanted music to which people had really responded; records put on sale that at least somebody thought were worth paying for."[45]

"Our Bible"

The songs were arranged not chronologically or in standard categories but in three catchall divisions: Ballads, Social Music, and Songs. The arrangement seemed at first arbitrary, but in fact was deliberate and subtle; the words

In 1952 Harry Smith (pictured in 1987) released the Anthology of American Folk Music, *a collection of early American folk songs.*

In the Public Eye Again

Many songs that became popular during the folk boom were in the public domain; no author was listed and so no royalties had to be paid to composers. Sometimes songs that did have specific authors were never even properly credited. An exception to this neglect was a big hit for the Rooftop Singers, "Walk Right In."

The group sought out the writer, Memphis jug band legend Gus Cannon, and paid him five hundred dollars plus 25 percent of the royalties. Cannon, who had been living in obscurity and working as a gardener, further benefited from the song's popularity by being able to tour with other older musicians on the revived folk circuit.

or music of a given song echoed the one before it and foreshadowed the one to come, linking all the songs in unexpected ways.

One intriguing aspect of the *Anthology* was that its performers were not identified by race anywhere in the package. Smith thus deliberately blurred the listener's racial preconceptions. Long after the collection's release, he remarked with satisfaction about a black bluesman, "It was years before anybody discovered that Mississippi John Hurt wasn't a hillbilly."[46]

The release of the *Anthology* electrified the folk music scene. Devotees pored over its puzzling notes and eccentric song choices. For them it was a tantalizing glimpse into what Marcus calls the lost world of "the old, weird America."[47]

The *Anthology* thus became an essential cornerstone of every folkie's education. This was especially true for younger musicians like Van Ronk, who remarks that it was "our Bible. We all knew every word of every song in it, including the ones we hated."[48]

Of course, Smith's collection was not solely responsible for inspiring young performers like Van Ronk to explore and expand the folk music movement. It was simply an important inspiration. Other factors were also at play as a new generation brought the folk revival to its full blossoming.

Chapter Six

The Folk Boom

The folk boom made media heroes and political stars of artists, spurred research into every area of traditional American music and culture, and made owning a guitar a rite of passage for millions of adolescents.

—writer Phil Hood, *Artists of American Folk Music*

College students and other young people were largely responsible for the second phase of the folk revival. During this period, which lasted roughly from 1958 to 1965, folk became a national craze. A younger generation carried on the postwar revival begun by earlier folkies, expanding both the definition of the music and its audience.

Part of folk's appeal to these young people was its emphasis on naturalness and authenticity; as the world seemed to grow increasingly complex, traditional music's acoustic instruments and lack of pretense continued to hold the promise of a simpler, happier time. Singer and songwriter Tom Rush commented, "It sounded real—it sounded like real people playing wooden things and without a lot of prettying-up and fancy arrangements. . . . We'd go out and find these ancient records and play them, and the guitars sounded out of tune, and you couldn't understand the words. But it was more powerful than anything you'd hear anywhere else."[49]

Traditional folk's younger cousin, protest music, also appealed to many college-age fans. (The term came into use during this time to describe topical political songs.) To them, protest music was an important way of addressing such increasingly dire political upheavals as poverty, conflicts over the atomic bomb, and the civil rights movement.

The Kingston Trio

Some folk enthusiasts during this period were purists who insisted on listening to only the most authentic performances. (Devotees of Smith's *Anthol-*

ogy were generally part of this group.) However, the Weavers' success had demonstrated that there was also strong interest for a smoother, more pop-oriented folk sound.

Inevitably, the music industry met that need, and the result was an explosion in commercial folk. One particular group was responsible for launching this fad: three young men from the San Francisco Bay Area called the Kingston Trio. The group's

The Kingston Trio, Bob Shane, Dave Guard (standing), and Nick Reynolds, were the first commercially successful folk music band.

cheerful demeanor and neat appearance made them attractive to mass audiences, a style that was both cheered and jeered. Writer Phil Hood notes: "The Kingston Trio gets credit (and the blame) for launching the most commercial phase of the urban folk boom."[50]

The group scored its first hit in 1958 with "Tom Dooley." This was an updated version of "Tom Dula," an old ballad about a Civil War–era murderer on the eve of his hanging. With its three-part harmony and vaguely Caribbean beat, the Kingston Trio's version of this sad song was easy to listen to; it sold over 3 million copies and won a Grammy award.

Hootenannies Everywhere

The runaway success of "Tom Dooley" and the group's many follow-up hits transformed the music scene. For decades folk had been a marginal genre in commercial terms; suddenly, the recording industry was desperately seeking folkies with sales potential. Prominent among the many who followed in the Kingston Trio's wake were the Chad Mitchell Trio, the Wayfarers, the Brothers Four, the New Christy Minstrels, Burl Ives, the Limeliters, and the Serendipity Singers.

The craze blossomed in other ways as well. For example, informal singing and song-swap sessions were held frequently in parks and other gathering places across the country. The term "hootenanny"—used to describe these sessions—became a household word.

The New Christy Minstrels benefited from the burgeoning success of folk music during the 1960s.

(The word's origin is unclear, though apparently Seeger and Guthrie first popularized it in the 1940s.)

Thousands of students across the country joined campus folk clubs or hung out at folk nightclubs. One estimate claimed that a million acoustic guitars were being sold every year to aspiring folk musicians. Manufacturers of other products jumped on the bandwagon as well: The word "hootenanny" was used to sell items as diverse as sweatshirts, candy bars, doll clothes, bath powders, pinball machines, shoes, paper dolls, and even an amusement park in New Jersey. (It sponsored a Miss Hootenanny contest.) No one knew exactly why folk caught on so strongly; the trade newspaper *Show Business* headlined one article "Folk Music Craze Baffles Experts."[51]

Nothing Without It

What would American music be, singer Bonnie Raitt reflects, without traditional folk music?

American roots music is at the center of this country's soul. Without roots music, there would be no American music or modern popular culture today. No jazz, no rhythm & blues, no pop music, no rock & roll. No Beatles, no Rolling Stones, no MTV, no rap. Field hollers, work songs, and the old folksongs that people brought with them from the British Isles—these are the earliest sounds of our musical heritage and the source of the many great musical forms that would follow.

Quoted in Robert Santelli, Holly George-Warren, and Jim Brown, eds., *American Roots Music*. New York: Abrams, 2001, p. 8.

Of course, not everyone was wild about the music. Many older people, in particular, disdained it as a silly fad. In his syndicated newspaper column, writer Earl Wilson sneered, "About all you need to be a singer nowadays is a guitar and a cold in the head."[52]

Traditionalists

And, of course, not every young folk enthusiast applauded the music's commercial side. A devoted minority preferred music out of the mainstream. These fans doggedly sought out unusual or obscure strains of traditional folk, in the process discovering (or rediscovering) many classic musicians. As a result, Jabbour notes, "Eventually the revival touched virtually every ethnic tradition resident in America."[53]

There were many examples. The New Lost City Ramblers (a trio including Mike Seeger, Pete's half-brother) kept old-time string band music alive with intensely authentic performances. Theodore Bikel focused on Jewish folk songs. Richard Dyer-Bennett concentrated on British ballads sung in a style influenced by European minstrels, and John Jacob Niles performed Appalachian ballads in an eerie but mesmerizing voice. A number of young performers, including Van Ronk, focused on blues traditions, emulating and championing such older blues masters as Son House, Mississippi John Hurt, and Skip James.

Not every folk revivalist was strictly commercial or strictly traditionalist; some fell between the cracks. For example, the Jim Kweskin Jug Band was a Boston "good time music" group that gained fame for its notably eccentric versions of old string band numbers. Member Geoff Muldaur once remarked, "If we couldn't murder a song, we weren't interested in it."[54]

A National Scene

The folk boom, in both commercial and purist modes, was in full swing by the early 1960s. Radio stations and colleges began featuring regular folk shows. Hundreds of folk albums were released as well—more than two hundred just in the year 1963.

But the most popular venues for live music were clubs or coffee shops. These were direct descendants of a fad of the 1950s: coffee shops that featured jazz and poetry, the favored entertainment of the beatnik movement. A handful of coffee shops featuring folk had been around earlier, but their numbers and popularity soared in the wake of "Tom Dooley." Almost every city of any size had at least one, usually featuring (in addition to the music, of course) low lights, funky furnishings, and strong coffee.

Many prominent performers launched national careers from these local clubs. The Kingston Trio's first major engagement was at San Francisco's Purple Onion. Jim (Roger) McGuinn, soon to be a key figure in folk music's evolution, got his big break at Los Angeles' Troubadour. And Joan Baez—whose pure soprano voice, gentle appearance, and fierce political views would soon make her one of folk's great icons—debuted at Club 47 in Cambridge, Massachusetts.

The New York City Scene

But the undisputed center of the folk revival was New York City. It boasted the most prestigious clubs and was home to famous radio shows like Brand's "Folk Song Festival." New York was also the center for influential folk-oriented magazines like *Sing Out!* and *Broadside*, as well as folkie record labels such as Folkways and Elektra.

Joan Baez, a folk music icon, plays guitar on the beach in 1962.

Folk singer Phil Ochs performs in New York City's Central Park in 1975.

Washington Square Park, the scene of regular open-air hootenannies.

At one time or another the Village was home to many established artists, including Seeger, Guthrie, Lead Belly, and such contemporaries of theirs as Ramblin' Jack Elliott, Cisco Houston, and Odetta. In addition, dozens of younger folk singers and songwriters made the Village their home. Baez and Van Ronk were prominent among these younger performers; others included Phil Ochs, Tom Paxton, Mark Spoelstra, Judy Collins, and the trio of Peter, Paul, and Mary.

Protest Music

These younger Village musicians (and their compatriots around the country) played a major role in redefining folk music. On the one hand, they embraced folk's traditional aspects. But they were also writing and performing new songs—edgy, often angry compositions about social injustice.

This protest music was a far cry from the relatively carefree and apolitical topics of traditional ballads. Protest songs hearkened back instead to the days of the broadsides and of the social issue songs of the 1930s and 1940s. A writer for *Time* magazine noted, "All over the U.S., folk singers are doing what folk singers are classically supposed to do—singing about current crises. . . . Instead of keening over the poor old cowpoke who died in the streets of Laredo . . . they are singing with hot-eyed fervor about police dogs and racial murder."[55]

The vibrant heart of this scene was Greenwich Village. For many decades this neighborhood had sheltered New York's community of artists, writers, and musicians, and now it was overrun with folk musicians. Singers and fans hung out at Village coffeehouses like Gerde's Folk City and the Bitter End. They spent money (if they had it) at Izzy Young's Folklore Center, an instrument and record shop that served as the community's main meeting place. And they checked each other out in

"A Woody Guthrie Jukebox"

Of all the Village protest musicians, one stood out. Bob Dylan was a boyish, curly haired singer with a nasal voice. But he was also a charismatic figure and a brilliant songwriter. The combination was potent; writer David McGee notes that Dylan was gifted with "vivid, eloquent, socially conscious writing and an untrained voice that carried a tremendous emotional wallop."[56]

Judy Collins, an artist from New York's Village folk music scene, performs onstage in 1966.

Music Everywhere

The traditional folk movement, in all its many forms, is very much alive and well today. Music writer Bill C. Malone comments:

Throughout America, thousands of people play music on weekends, or even during the week, and then go to their day jobs. . . . They have never been able to give up their wage-earning occupations (some in fact work only to support their love of music). Still others participate in weekly jam sessions at someone's house or at the local VFW or American Legion Hall. Others take part in fiddle contests or festivals or play in church or at local barn dances. Some take time out each year to learn traditional music arts at workshops or through instructional tapes or videos. This truly down-home form of music making *is* roots music, and as long as this kind of democratic participation persists, [styles such as] country music will endure and remain healthy.

Bill C. Malone, "Keeping It Country: Tradition and Change, 1940 to the Present," in *American Roots Music*, eds. Robert Santelli, Holly George-Warren, and Jim Brown. New York: Abrams, 2001, p. 177.

Born Robert Zimmerman, Dylan had discovered folk music as a teenager in small-town Minnesota. He was especially enamored of Guthrie's music and personal style. The younger musician began aping his idol's folksy drawl and scruffy clothes, and he learned every Guthrie tune he could; Dylan later described himself during this period as "a Woody Guthrie jukebox."[57]

Arriving in New York, Dylan made several pilgrimages to visit his idol, who was slowly dying in a New Jersey hospital. Dylan also immersed himself in the Village scene. It was rough going at first—he had such an abrasive voice that, according to legend, one club owner let him onstage only when he wanted to clear the house.

Eventually, though, Dylan's poetic, intense songs attracted attention. Among them were "Blowin' in the Wind," "Only a Pawn in Their Game," and "A Hard Rain's A-Gonna Fall." Dylan and Baez (who were linked romantically for a time) emerged as the undisputed king and queen of the new folk movement.

Festivals

Television networks took notice of the blossoming movement, and in the spring of 1963 a nationally broadcast show, *Hootenanny*, debuted. At its peak the program attracted millions of viewers weekly, but it was hampered by a lack of high-quality acts. Seeger, who had helped introduce the very word "hootenanny," was banned from the show—a remnant of the Red Scare era. Many top performers, including Baez and Dylan, refused to appear as a result; with only second-string performers on hand, the show lasted only two seasons.

The folk festivals of this period were more durable. The biggest and most

Standout protest musician Bob Dylan accompanies himself with guitar and harmonica.

prestigious of these was an annual event in Newport, Rhode Island. The first Newport festival, in 1959, drew a crowd of fifteen thousand, and it grew steadily more popular in later years.

Newport became an important venue for introducing to a wide audience unknown musicians from many traditions. Among the many performers who received national attention after appearances there were Doc Watson, a blind guitarist and singer from North Carolina; the Balfa Brothers, Cajun musicians from southwest Louisiana; and such blues masters as Son House, Mississippi John Hurt, Lightnin' Hopkins, and Sleepy John Estes.

Newport was also an important proving ground for young musicians. The first festival in 1959, for instance, introduced Baez to audiences beyond the Boston area; she emerged as a major artist after an electrifying performance of only two ballads sung in duet with a more established singer, Bob Gibson. Brand, who was master of ceremonies, recalls, "It was the whole atmosphere of the occasion. . . . It had been raining. Her hair was stringing down her face. And she stood there very, very simply, and the intensity with which she performed in front of that audience of thousands was just tremendous. It was like she had an aura around her."[58]

Dylan Goes Electric

Newport was responsible for another pivotal moment in folk music history. In 1965 Dylan, the movement's most prominent performer, made a radical decision: He went electric. Inspired by the arrival of the Beatles the year before, Dylan was convinced that he could merge folk with rock and—never shy of publicity or controversy—chose the prominent Newport festival as his public debut.

In the years since, Dylan's performance has achieved legendary status. He took the stage in a black leather jacket and was joined by a band that included members of Chicago's Paul Butterfield Blues Band. The group had been rehearsing in secret all night before the show.

Without an introduction, it launched into a raucous version of Dylan's song "Maggie's Farm." Seeger, who was backstage, was aghast. According to some accounts, he was so incensed by the band's volume that he threatened to chop their amplifier cables with an axe.

Dylan walked off after only three songs, with much of the crowd booing. The crowd may have been angry at the electric instruments, the radically different music, the brevity of the set, the musicians' lack of polish, the bad sound system (which was not set up for electric instruments), or some combination of these factors. To Muldaur, who was there, people were simply annoyed with the quality of the music: "I don't believe people were booing because the music was revolutionary. It was just that Dylan wasn't very good at it. He had no idea how to play the electric guitar, and he had very second-rate

"Anguish, Confusion, and Charges of Betrayal"

Dylan's famous electric performance at Newport did not end the folk revival, but, folklorist Alan Jabbour writes, it was a signal that the folk movement was undergoing an identity crisis.

S ome argued that 1965 was really the turning point. The movement valued above all else the intimacy of personal expression, created by soloists and small ensembles; though the folk revival sometimes mobilized large crowds, its soul was found in intimate gathering and informal sing-alongs. . . . The revival always put a premium on acoustic instruments and defined itself as nonelectrified—not plugged in. Thus, by some accounts, the revival ended when Dylan went electric. [His] legendary appearance at Newport in 1965 . . . with shrieking electric guitar, harsh vocal delivery, and daunting volume [provoked] anguish, confusion, and charges of betrayal from the revival community.

Alan Jabbour, "The Flowering of the Folk Revival," in *American Roots Music*, eds. Robert Santelli, Holly George-Warren, and Jim Brown. New York: Abrams, 2001, p. 75.

Bob Dylan, pictured playing electric guitar, caused a stir when he switched from acoustic to electric.

musicians with him, and they hadn't rehearsed enough. It just didn't work. . . . There's no doubt in my mind, people were booing because it stank."[59]

A Shift

Dylan returned with just his acoustic guitar to finish the set. But he had laid down his challenge. Dylan's bold act polarized the folk movement, and its impact was felt for years.

Purists who revered acoustic instruments and traditional ways were horrified; Seeger, for his part, called Dylan's performance "some of the most destructive music this side of hell."[60] Others, not as devoted to old customs, found the merger of folk and rock thrilling. And still others were simply mystified or disappointed, feeling that Dylan's performance had been more inappropriate than earthshaking. Summing up these feelings, Bikel remarked, "You don't whistle in church—you don't play rock and roll at a folk festival."[61]

Dylan going electric did not kill the folk revival. It did, however, symbolize a major shift in the music. In the next few years folk would indeed blend with rock and inspire a number of intriguing musical developments. The folk boom was ending, but a new era was beginning.

Chapter Seven

Recent Developments

Folk music has never been close to extinction. . . This has always been a singing country, stimulated by constant injections of new songs and new ideas.
—singer and radio host Oscar Brand, *The Ballad-Mongers*

To a degree, the folk boom faded away in the mid- and late 1960s, as musical styles tend to do. Folk never went completely away, however; it just evolved. The music thus demonstrated, as it had in the past, its adaptability to new times and circumstances.

One change was a shift in the emphasis of protest music. As protests over civil rights and Vietnam became less of a concern, activists largely turned elsewhere. Many, like Seeger with his campaign to clean up the Hudson River, began focusing on environmental issues.

Probably the most important change in folk during this period, however, was the merger with rock that Dylan had helped to pioneer. This hybrid style was given a new name: folk-rock. Musi-cally, folk-rock mixed acoustic with electric instruments, with bass and drums providing a beat. Lyrically, it combined the storytelling power of traditional folk, the political awareness of protest music, and the poetic imagery and strong rhythms of rock.

Out on Highway 61

Dylan was the music's undisputed champion. Even before Newport, Dylan had spliced acoustic and electric instruments on part of his album *Bringing It All Back Home*. His next albums— *Highway 61 Revisited* and *Blonde on Blonde*, which followed his Newport appearance—were further milestones in the development of folk-rock.

They had a distinctive and robust sound, one that set the standard for virtually every folk-rocker to come. His live performances, backed by a group called the Hawks (later known simply as the Band), were similarly galvanizing. As writers Larry Sandberg and Dick Weissman remark, Dylan's emergence

Finding Good Barbecue in Maine

Folk culture, including music, is so much a part of everyday life that it can be nearly overlooked. Despite inroads made by such inventions as television, radio, recordings, and the Internet, it remains still regional to a degree. Music writer Kip Lornell notes:

Our participation in folk culture is almost subconscious or second nature. These are the customs and traditions that we learn or assimilate from our family, members of the community, and our ethnic or racial group. Folk culture can be expressed in myriad ways—how we celebrate our religious holidays, greet one another, or pronounce certain words. It is unofficial and non-institutional, and we live it in many ways, including what we eat. For example, good pulled-pork barbecue is all but impossible to find in Rangley, Maine, but not difficult to locate in Bossier City, Louisiana.

Kip Lornell, *The NPR Curious Listener's Guide to American Folk*. New York: Berkley Perigee, 2004, pp. 3–4.

from the folk scene into the glare of rock stardom opened the door for others to experiment similarly:

Dylan's success made it commercially and artistically respectable for folk-rooted artists to use electric sounds, and for pop artists to use acoustic–folk sounds and to draw on traditional styles and materials. Dylan also made it possible for songwriters to express a whole range of emotions and social attitudes that previously had not been commercially viable.[62]

The Byrds and More

Dylan may have been the king of folk-rock, but he was not its only pioneer. A British band, the Animals, had a hit in 1965 with its version of a traditional American ballad, "House of the Rising Sun." And then there was a Los Angeles band, the Byrds.

Like the Animals and Dylan's rock debut, the Byrds burst on the scene in 1965. The distinctive sound of their first number-one hit (a version of Dylan's "Mr. Tambourine Man") was built around the chiming twelve-string guitar and bittersweet vocals of McGuinn, a veteran of such earlier folk groups as the Limeliters and the Chad Mitchell Trio. The group followed this first hit with another equally successful song (Seeger's "Turn, Turn, Turn") and went on to become the first rock band to seriously challenge the popularity of the Beatles.

Inspired by Dylan and the Byrds, folkies all across the country went electric. One notable group was a San Francisco bluegrass band, Mother McCree's Uptown Jug Champions. When the group switched direction, it changed its name to the Grateful Dead

Electric folk group the Byrds helped to popularize folk-rock in the mid-1960s.

—and became one of the most popular and influential bands in rock history.

More Folk-Rockers

There were many more examples of the folk-rock connection. Janis Joplin, the powerhouse singer for a seminal San Francisco band, Big Brother & the Holding Company, had deep roots in the Texas blues and folk scene. The Lovin' Spoonful, from New York, mixed rock with elements of good-time string band music. Buffalo Springfield, a Los Angeles band, was short-lived but influential, launching the careers of such future stars as Stephen Stills and Neil Young.

When folk-rock developed outside of established music centers, it often had a distinctly regional flavor. In Texas, for instance, a mixed Hispanic/Anglo group, the Sir Douglas Quintet, played an energetic mixture of blues, *norteño*, and rock. The influence

Los Angeles folk-rock group Buffalo Springfield launched the career of Neil Young (far right).

of the folk-rock movement extended far beyond America as well; in England, for example, bands like Pentangle and Fairport Convention established their own vibrant scene.

In the late 1960s folk and rock combined in yet a new way, adding a strong element of traditional country music. Both the Byrds and Dylan led this movement, resulting in albums like the Byrds' *Sweetheart of the Rodeo* and Dylan's *Nashville Skyline*. Meanwhile, Dylan's former backup group, the Band, released *Music from Big Pink*, the first of many intelligent and musically rich albums incorporating country, blues, gospel, and more.

The Blues Bounces Back

In the early fifties American folk styles had caught on in England, fueled in part by a radio series Alan Lomax had helped produce. This created, among other things, a uniquely British style called skiffle. The skiffle craze had inspired a number of young musicians—including teenagers John Lennon and Paul McCartney—to form their first bands.

The blues also captivated many young British musicians, including Van Morrison, Eric Clapton, and the members of the Rolling Stones. They revered American bluesmen—the Rolling Stones, for instance, were named after a Muddy Waters song. The Stones and other English musicians then reintroduced the blues to America when they stormed the country in the mid- to late 1960s as part of the British

Singer-songwriter Joni Mitchell plays a mountain dulcimer in 1970.

Invasion, the massive influx of bands that followed the Beatles' success.

Previously, mainstream American audiences had ignored the blues; now, however, millions of young British Invasion fans had a chance to understand that it was a vital part of their heritage. Not every fan made the connection, of course, even though many bands made it explicit. Nonetheless, the seeds were planted; Filene notes, "The notion of the Chicago blues as a roots music was taking hold."[63]

Singer-Songwriters

After the British Invasion and throughout the 1970s, folk music continued to evolve and expand. Increasingly, this occurred in separate (and sometimes overlapping) ways. As both the music industry and its audience grew larger, folk fractured into a number of distinct categories—and has continued to do so.

One instance is how the classic folksinger morphed into a new form of musician loosely categorized as the singer-songwriter. Guthrie and Dylan can be considered early prototypes for this genre. However, it reached a peak with 1970s stars like Joni Mitchell, James Taylor, and Simon and Garfunkel.

As the name implies, singer-songwriters specialized in performing their own compositions. Lyrically these songs tended to be folk-influenced and intensely introspective. Musically their work was more electric and pop-oriented than older, "true" folkies, blending elements of many different styles. Writer Bill C. Malone notes, "Like Dylan, who has influenced them all, these singers have freely fused the sounds of country, rock, and folk to

Lucinda Williams is one of many current performers extending and deepening the singer-songwriter tradition.

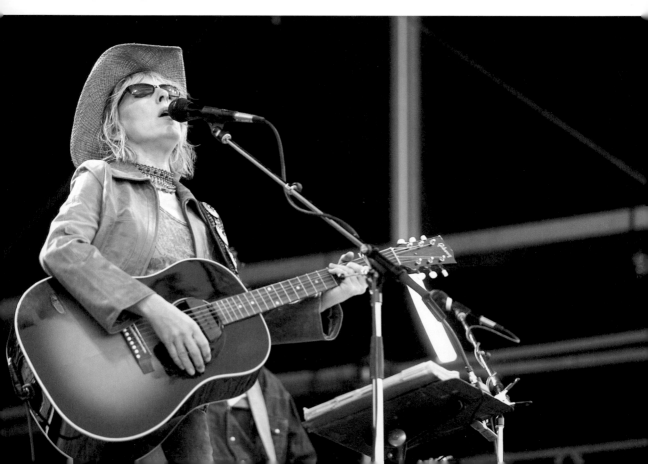

Emmylou Harris (left) is a prominent contemporary singer whose roots are in coutnry music, while Bonnie Raitt (right) traces her roots to the rural blues tradition.

create songs that comment intelligently on the human condition."[64]

The singer-songwriter tradition continues to evolve and thrive. The long list of prominent current performers includes John Prine, Lucinda Williams, Tracy Chapman, Greg Brown, Dar Williams, Jesse Winchester, John Hiatt, Lyle Lovett, Dave Matthews, Arlo Guthrie (Woody's son), and Shawn Colvin. Bruce Springsteen, famous as a rocker, also has made explicit his affinity with Woody Guthrie–style folk through such introspective albums as *Devils & Dust.*

New Branches

Closely related to the singer-songwriter is the folk-influenced interpreter of songs (as opposed to those who write most of their own material). The many current examples of this style include Emmylou Harris, Maura O'Connell, and Nanci Griffith. Another standout is Bonnie Raitt, who began her career as a devotee of rural blues performers like Sippie Wallace and Fred McDowell and has since evolved into a distinctive singer and slide guitarist.

Some performers, although clearly folk-influenced, refuse to fall into neat categories. Since his days with the Jim Kweskin Jug Band, Muldaur has released a string of quirky, innovative albums mixing blues, jazz, and old-time string band music. Singer Gillian Welch and her guitarist and songwriting partner David Rawlings perform what she calls "American Primitive," setting elements of bluegrass and mountain music against Welch's eerie, old-timey voice.

Still another aspect of the folk-derived music scene revolves around the evolution of country-rock. The 1960s music of groups like the Byrds became in the 1970s a slick, commercial sound typified by such bands as Poco and the Eagles. More recently, it has evolved into an inventive style called alt.country, typified by bands like Uncle Tupelo, Wilco, and Son Volt.

Bluegrass also remains alive and well, having spawned such creative offshoots as "progressive bluegrass" and "newgrass." These styles mix traditional bluegrass with jazz and other innovative sounds. Among the many practitioners

Innovative bluegrass musician Alison Krauss plays fiddle at a 2005 music festival.

"These Sounds . . . Are America"

Individual songs or musical styles, heard together over time, form a continuous stream of rich tradition. Robert Santelli comments:

The sounds are as sweet as mountain air: the lonesome drift of a fiddle, the easy pluck of banjo strings, the wailing notes from a harmonica, a romping guitar chord, the thump of a homemade drum, a vocal moan. On the surface they seem so simple, even fleeting, as if they were created to celebrate only the moment or to capture a particular emotion, like love or loss. Yet almost always they're drawn from a deeper place and, when bound together, become part of a powerful tradition. These sounds, in all their variety and beauty, are America.

Robert Santelli, "Introduction," in *American Roots Music*, eds. Robert Santelli, Holly George-Warren, and Jim Brown. New York: Abrams, 2001, p. 12.

of this genre are mandolinists David Grisman and Sam Bush, banjo virtuoso Béla Fleck, fiddler-singer Alison Krauss, and the ensemble Nickel Creek.

More Branches

Today's folk traditions extend into many more branches as well, such as the blues. Among the most prominent performers in this genre are Keb' Mo', Tracy Nelson, John Hammond Jr., Susan Tedeschi, and Robert Cray. Another is Taj Mahal, who—over a long and prolific career—has creatively mined many of the music's rich veins, including its connections with African and Caribbean music.

Meanwhile, Mexican American folk–derived music continues to evolve. For example, the *corrido*—the heroic ballad—was reinvigorated in the 1960s, due partly to the assassination of John F. Kennedy (dozens of songs about him were recorded and broadcast), and partly to the Chicano movement (which fostered pride in Mexican American culture and inspired *corridos* about social leaders and cultural pride). More recently, songs called *narcocorridos* have sprung up; Los Tigres del Norte are the most famous performers of these musical chronicles of drug traffickers and gangsters.

The soundtrack from the film O Brother, Where Art Thou? *includes songs by the fictional trio the Soggy Bottom Boys (pictured). The film helped revitalize interest in folk music.*

Like other folk-derived styles in the 1960s, *norteño*, traditional Tex-Mex dance music, adopted electric instruments and drums. The popularity of accordion virtuoso Flaco Jiménez in the 1980s then brought *norteño* to a vast new audience. Adding to this were contributions from rock star Linda Ronstadt (who recorded two gorgeous albums celebrating her part-Mexican heritage), singer-songwriter Tish Hinojosa, the rock band Los Lobos, and the changing collective of superstars called Los Super Seven.

"O Brother" and More

In addition to these performers, movies have helped keep folk alive as well. Films about folk music include the documentaries of Les Blank (about Cajun

music and other forms) as well as documentaries about the Greenwich Village scene and other aspects of the music's history. Perhaps the most prominent folk-related film, however, is the Coen Brothers' *O Brother, Where Art Thou?*

This 2000 comedy, which stars George Clooney, is set in the Deep South during the 1930s and tells the story of three bumbling prison escapees trying to get home. Along the way they find unexpected fame (after disguising themselves as a string band called the Soggy Bottom Boys). The film makes use of several musical styles, in particular hillbilly music, and its success inspired a concert tour, a documentary film, and two award-winning CDs featuring performers such as Harris,

Welch, Krauss, Ralph Stanley, and the gospel group The Fairfield Four.

Another aspect of the continuing interest in folk music is Smith's famous set of recordings, the *Anthology of American Music*. Reissued on CD in 1997, the collection boasts extensive new notes by music scholars and a CD-ROM of extra material. The *Anthology* continues to inspire musicians and listeners more than a half-century after its original release helped launch the folk boom.

More Recordings

Yet another recording project is a massive ongoing series from Rounder Records, projected to include 150 CDs, that will encompass all of Alan Lomax's historic recordings. Further projects include other reissues of seminal folk recordings, as well as tribute albums by contemporary performers. Among the latter are CDs honoring the Carter Family, Lead Belly, Guthrie, Hurt, Seeger, Dylan, and Rodgers.

The pioneers of the folk movement continue to influence the recordings of contemporary performers as well. For instance, the alt.country band Wilco collaborated in the late 1990s with the politically minded British folk singer Billy Bragg on a brilliant pair of albums, *Mermaid Avenue* (vols. I and II), setting a group of Guthrie's unrecorded lyrics to new music. And the premiere band of the grunge era, Nirvana, recorded a Lead Belly tune ("Where Did You Sleep Last Night?") on an album released in 1994.

Passing It On Today

Strictly speaking, traditional music is transmitted from one performer to another; people learn by hearing a song performed live frequently over the years. However, this is not always the case today, as Larry Sandberg and Dick Weissman note:

Music in traditional style, as played nowadays, is learned for the most part from records, often with some auxiliary use of books. The musicians are not from the older, fast-disappearing folk culture. . . . Many have taken the trouble to develop an acquaintance or even friendship with older musicians, but their position is more like that of an anthropologist in the field than that of a genuine member of the culture.

Larry Sandberg and Dick Weissman, *The Folk Music Sourcebook*. New York: Da Capo, 1989, p. 107.

British folk singer Billy Bragg (left) recorded two critically-acclaimed albums of new songs set to unrecorded lyrics by folk-icon Woody Guthrie.

In addition to such recordings, recognition of major folk music figures has come from many other directions. For example, Lead Belly, Guthrie, Waters, Seeger, and Dylan have all been inducted into the Rock and Roll Hall of Fame.

Government Recognition

Recognition by the government has also played an important part in keeping folk alive and vital. Sometimes this has taken the form of specific honors. For instance, Waters, Guthrie, and Lead Belly were all honored with U.S. postal stamps as part of the Legends of American Music series.

Further official honors include National Medals of the Arts for Lomax (1986) and Seeger (1994). Seeger (in 1994) and Dylan (in 1997) each received Kennedy Center Honors. And Lomax's book *The Land Where the Blues Began* won the National Book Critics Circle award in 1993.

Sometimes, the role of government has involved the passage of legislation. In 1976, for instance, Congress passed the American Folklife Preservation Act. Among other things, this law has helped fund the American Folklife Center at the Library of Congress. This center preserves and promotes many forms of American folk culture, including music.

More recently, the inauguration of President Bill Clinton and Vice President Al Gore inspired a festival in Washington, D.C., that attracted an estimated half-million visitors to celebrate the diversity of America's folk music. At the time, Clinton and Gore commented on the importance of this variety: "Just as the creativity, genius and generosity of individuals enlarges our sense of humanity, so too can an appreciation of our diversity increase our sense of national accomplishment." [65]

Folk festivals, government-sponsored or not, remain popular; hundreds are held every year across the country. Some, such as the traditional fiddling festival in Union Grove, North Carolina, focus on regional styles or individual instruments. Others are broader in scope, celebrating styles from around the country and the world. One prominent example is the annual Folklife Festival in Seattle, Washington, believed to be the largest free festival of its kind in the country.

The Legacy

It seems clear that folk music in its many forms is in no danger of dying out. It might be traditional or modern, played on quiet acoustic instruments or with loud electric ones. It might be raucous blues or sweet ballads, biting protest music or gentle love songs. It might be sung in any of several tongues, with ancient melodies or up-to-the-moment language. In whatever form it takes, folk is still being played, enjoyed, and tinkered with everywhere. Botkin notes, "Folklore is not something far away and long ago, but real and living among us." [66]

Furthermore, folk music is no longer confined to an obscure corner of the musical map. It is part of everyday life for virtually all Americans, who can hear folk influences not just in popular music but in radio and TV commercials and movie scores. As Sandberg and Weissman note, "The ring of the five-string banjo and the bluesy twang of the slide guitar . . . have entered the cultural mainstream." [67]

The folk music Americans enjoy today, in all its myriad shapes and forms, is the fruit of a century of revivalism and innovation. It is also the fruit of the many centuries of music that came before. Folk music will not soon lose its power to entertain and inspire.

• Notes •

Introduction: "Music That Falls Between the Cracks"

1. Alan Jabbour, "The Flowering of the Folk Revival," in *American Roots Music*, eds. Robert Santelli, Holly George-Warren, and Jim Brown. New York: Abrams, 2001, p. 58.
2. Quoted in Kip Lornell, *The NPR Curious Listener's Guide to American Folk*. New York: Berkley Perigee, 2004, p. xiii.
3. David Hajdu, *Positively 4ᵗʰ Street: The Lives and Times of Joan Baez, Bob Dylan, Mimi Baez Fariña, and Richard Fariña*. New York: Farrar, Straus and Giroux, 2001, p. 10.
4. Quoted in Benjamin Filene, *Romancing the Folk: Public Memory and American Roots Music*. Chapel Hill: University of North Carolina Press, 2000, p. 52.
5. Quoted in Filene, *Romancing the Folk*, p. 138.
6. Roger D. Abrahams and George Foss, *Anglo American Folksong Style*. Englewood Cliffs, NJ: Prentice Hall, 1968, p. 1.
7. Oscar Brand, *The Ballad Mongers: Rise of the Modern Folk Song*. Westport, CT: Greenwood, 1962, p. 49.

Chapter One: British Folk in the New World

8. Abrahams and Foss, *Anglo-American Folksong Style*, p. 12.
9. Hugh Blumenfeld, "Folk Music 101, Part II: Origins of Folk Music," Hugh Blumenfeld: Singer-Songwriter. www.hughblumenfeld.com.
10. Samuel L. Forcucci, *A Folk Song History of America*. Englewood Cliffs, NJ: Prentice Hall, 1984, p. 35.
11. Blumenfeld, "Folk Music 101, Part II."

Chapter Two: African American Roots

12. Quoted in Timothy White, *Rock Lives*. New York: Henry Holt, 1990, p. 720.
13. Robert Darden, *People Get Ready! A New History of Black Gospel Music*. New York: Continuum, 2004, p. 1.
14. Quoted in Dena J. Epstein, *Sinful Tunes and Spirituals: Black Folk Music to the Civil War*. Urbana: University of Illinois Press, 1977, pp. 58–59.
15. Alan Lomax, *The Folk Songs of North America*. Garden City, NY: Doubleday, 1960, p. xix.
16. Epstein, *Sinful Tunes and Spirituals: Black Folk Music to the Civil War.*, p. 100.
17. James Weldon Johnson, "Negro Folk Songs and Spirituals," repr., Document Records. www.document-records.com/index.asp?content=http://www.document-records.com/content_show_article.asp?id=189&offset=90.

18. Quoted in Viv Broughton, *Black Gospel: An Illustrated History of the Gospel Sound*. Poole, UK: Blandford, 1985, p. 32.
19. Bill Flanagan, *Written in My Soul*. Chicago: Contemporary Books, 1986, p. 9.

Chapter Three: New and Different Voices

20. Quoted in Robert Cantwell, *When We Were Good: The Folk Revival*. Cambridge, MA: Harvard University Press, 1996, pp. 33–34.
21. Ann Allen Savoy, "Cajun and Zydeco: The Musics of French Southwest Louisiana," in Santelli, George-Warren, and Brown, *American Roots Music*, p. 106.
22. Manuel Peña, "Música Tejana: The Music of Mexican Texas," in Santelli, George-Warren, and Brown, *American Roots Music*, p. 128.
23. Quoted in *Dan W. Dickey*, "Corridos," Texas Online. www.tsha. utexas.edu/handbook/online/ articles/CC/lhc1.html.
24. Quoted in Filene, *Romancing the Folk*, p. 34.
25. Forcucci, *A Folk Song History of America*, pp. 155–56.

Chapter Four: Folk Goes National

26. Lornell, *The NPR Curious Listener's Guide to American Folk*, p. 24.
27. Epstein, *Sinful Tunes and Spirituals*, p. 242.
28. Filene, *Romancing the Folk*, p. 35.
29. Bonnie Raitt, "Foreword," in Santelli, George-Warren, and Brown, *American Roots Music*, p. 8.

30. Dean Tudor and Nancy Tudor, *Grass Roots Music*. Littleton, CO: Libraries Unlimited, 1979, p. 132.
31. Quoted in Jon Pareles, "Alan Lomax, Who Raised Voice of Folk Music in U.S., Dies at 87," *New York Times*, July 23, 2002, repr., arsclist-NYT. http://palimpsest.stanford. edu/byform/mailing-lists/arsclist/ 2002/07/msg00049.html.
32. Quoted in Cantwell, *When We Were Good*, p. 73.
33. Quoted in Ronald D. Cohen, *Rainbow Quest: The Folk Music Revival and American Society, 1940–70*. Amherst: University of Massachusetts Press, 2002, p. 140.
34. Filene, *Romancing the Folk*, p. 107.
35. Quoted in Robert Santelli, "Mojo Working: The Blues Explosion," in Santelli, George-Warren, and Brown, *American Roots Music*, p. 192.
36. Cantwell, *When We Were Good*, 1996, p. 143.

Chapter Five: The Folk Revival Begins

37. Jabbour, "The Flowering of the Folk Revival," p. 58.
38. Quoted in Filene, *Romancing the Folk*, p. 188.
39. Quoted in Cohen, *Rainbow Quest*, p. 45.
40. Quoted in Brand, *The Ballad Mongers*, p. 80.
41. Quoted in Cantwell, *When We Were Good*, p. 179.
42. Quoted in Cohen, *Rainbow Quest*, p. 65.
43. Jabbour, "The Flowering of the Folk Revival," p. 65.

44. Dave Van Ronk with Elijah Wald, *The Mayor of MacDougall Street*. New York: Da Capo, 2005, p. 32.

45. Greil Marcus, "The Old, Weird America," notes accompanying *Anthology of American Folk Music*, audio CD, ed. Harry Smith, Smithsonian Folkways, 1997, p. 10.

46. Quoted in Cantwell, *When We Were Good*, p. 220.

47. Marcus, "The Old, Weird America," p. 1.

48. Quoted in Marcus, "The Old, Weird America," p. 5.

Chapter Six: The Folk Boom

49. Quoted in Hajdu, *Positively 4th Street*, p. 10.

50. Phil Hood, ed., "Introduction," in *Artists of American Folk Music*. New York: Morrow, 1986, p. 6.

51. Quoted in Hajdu, *Positively 4th Street*, p. 192.

52. Quoted in Brand, *The Ballad Mongers*, p. 105.

53. Jabbour, "The Flowering of the Folk Revival," p. 76.

54. Quoted in David McGee, "Roots Music Begats Rock & Roll," in Santelli, George-Warren, and Brown, *American Roots Music*, p. 226.

55. Quoted in Cohen, *Rainbow Quest*, pp. 204–05.

56. McGee, "Roots Music Begats Rock & Roll," p. 224.

57. Quoted in McGee, "Roots Music Begats Rock & Roll," p. 224.

58. Quoted in Hajdu, *Positively 4th Street*, p. 31.

59. Quoted in Hajdu, *Positively 4th Street*, p. 260.

60. Quoted in Filene, *Romancing the Folk*, p. 215.

61. Quoted in Filene, *Romancing the Folk*, p. 184.

Chapter Seven: Recent Developments

62. Larry Sandberg and Dick Weissman, *The Folk Music Sourcebook*. New York: Da Capo, 1989, p. 110.

63. Filene, *Romancing the Folk*, p. 123.

64. Bill C. Malone, "Keeping It Country: Tradition and Change, 1940 to the Present," in Santelli, George-Warren, and Brown, *American Roots Music*, p. 176.

65. Quoted in Filene, *Romancing the Folk*, p. 181.

66. Quoted in Filene, *Romancing the Folk*, p. 138.

67. Sandberg and Weissman, *The Folk Music Sourcebook*, p. x.

• For Further Reading •

Books

Oscar Brand, *The Ballad Mongers: Rise of the Modern Folk Song*. Westport, CT: Greenwood, 1962. A book by a central figure in the folk revival movement.

Jan Harold Brundvand, *American Folklore: An Encyclopedia*. New York: Garland, 1996. An encyclopedia of all manner of American folklore, with extensive entries on music.

Karen Mueller Coombs, *Woody Guthrie: America's Folksinger*. Minneapolis, MN: Carolrhoda, 2002. A well-written and illustrated biography of one of the folk scene's most important figures.

Bob Dylan, *Chronicles: Volume One*. New York: Simon & Schuster, 2004. Dylan has always been a master of disguise; this highly selective memoir, while entertaining, manages to keep much shrouded in mystery.

Bill Flanagan, *Written in My Soul*. Chicago: Contemporary Books, 1986. This volume focuses on some of rock and roll's best songwriters and has much to say about folk's influence on rock.

Woody Guthrie, *Bound for Glory*. New York: Plume, 1983. A reprint of a 1943 book, this colorful "autobiography" by the folk music icon is, in truth, probably closer to autobiographical fiction.

Phil Hood, ed., *Artists of American Folk Music*. New York: Morrow, 1986. Brief biographies of and interviews with some of folk's seminal figures by a variety of music writers.

Alan Lomax, *The Folk Songs of North America*. Garden City, NY: Doubleday, 1960. Annotated music and lyrics for over three hundred songs.

John A. Lomax and Alan Lomax, *American Songs and Folk Songs*. New York: Dover, 1994. A reprint of a classic 1934 annotated collection of songs by the distinguished father-son team of musicologists, based on their pioneering field recordings.

Kip Lornell, *The NPR Curious Listener's Guide to American Folk*. New York: Berkley Perigee, 2004. A useful short guide produced by National Public Radio.

Larry Sandberg and Dick Weissman, *The Folk Music Sourcebook*. New York: Da Capo, 1989. A useful guide to folk history, although its practical information is outdated.

Robert Santelli, Holly George-Warren, and Jim Brown, eds., *American Roots Music*. New York: Abrams, 2001. Great photos, a well-chosen range of essays, and information-packed prose highlight this guide based on the PBS TV series.

Peter Sieling, *Folk Music*. Broomall, PA: Mason Crest, 2003. Part of a series on North American folklore, this is a quick, breezily written overview of the subject.

———, *Folk Songs*. Broomall, PA: Mason Crest, 2003. A companion book to the author's more general volume on folk music.

Dave Van Ronk with Elijah Wald, *The Mayor of MacDougall Street*. New York: Da Capo, 2005. A fascinating memoir of the Greenwich Village folk scene by one of its key members.

Web Sites

The American Folklife Center at the Library of Congress (www.loc.gov/folklife). An informative site maintained by a distinguished branch of the national repository of folk music.

Ballad Tree: A Collection of Onsite Folk Music Information: Hugh Blumenfeld, editor (www.balladtree.com). This very extensive site, with essays both introductory and specialized, is maintained by a singer and songwriter.

The Great Folk Scare (www.zipcon.net/~highroad/folkscare.html). An entertaining and opinionated site dedicated to the history of the folk revival of the 1950s and 1960s.

NPR: America's Folk Music Anthology (www.npr.org/programs/morning/features/2002/jul/anthology). The online version of a National Public Radio report from 2002 on the ongoing influence of Harry Smith's collection.

WFMA Home Page (www.wfma.net). A site is maintained by the World Folk Music Association.

Recordings

Alan Lomax, Library of Congress/Rounder Records Recordings. This huge project, expected to eventually include 150 CDs, is reissuing Alan Lomax's seminal recordings of such performers as Woody Guthrie, Lead Belly, and such projects as the songs of coal miners, African American work songs, and Appalachian fiddle tunes.

Harry Smith, ed., *Anthology of American Folk Music*, Smithsonian Folkways, 1997. This six-CD reissue of the groundbreaking recordings compiled by the brilliant, eccentric Harry Smith includes both his own notes and more recent essays by other writers.

• Index •

guitar, 20, 21, 29, 30, 34, 44, 46, 52
guitarreros, 34
Guthrie, Arlo, 83
Guthrie, Woodrow Wilson (Woody), 10, 60–62, 68, 70, 72, 82, 83, 87, 88

Hackberry Ramblers (band), 52
Hajdu, David, 11
Hammond, John, Jr., 85
harmonica, 29, 30, 37
Harris, Emmylou, 83, 86
Hawks. *See* Band, The
Hayes, Alfred, 55
Hays, Lee, 57
Hebrides Islands (Scotland), 16
Hellerman, Fred, 57
Hiatt, John, 83
high lonesome (vocal style), 51
Highway 61 Revisited (album), 77
Hill Billies (musical group), 44
hillbilly music, 43–44, 46
Hinojosa, Tish, 86
"Home on the Range" (song), 48
Hood, Phil, 9, 65, 66
hootenannies, 67–68
Hootenanny (TV series), 73–74
Hopkins, Lightnin', 74
House, Son, 69, 74
"House Carpenter, The" (ballad), 16
"House of the Rising Sun" (ballad), 78
Houston, Cisco, 70
Hurt, Mississippi John, 64, 69, 74, 87
"Hush Little Baby" (lullaby), 21

"If I Had a Hammer" (song), 56
immigrants, 8, 31, 32, 39–40
"In the Jailhouse Now" (song), 48
"I Ride an Old Paint" (song), 38–39
Italian music, 40
"I've Been Working on the Railroad" (song), 36
Ives, Burl, 67
Izzy Young's Folklore Center (record shop), 70

Jabbour, Alan, 8, 61, 68, 75
James, Skip, 69
"Jam on Jerry's Rocks, The" (song), 36
"Jesse James" (song), 39
Jewish music, 40, 69
jigs, 14
Jiménez, Flaco, 86
Jim Kweskin Jug Band, 69, 84

"Joe Hill" (song), 55
"John Henry" (ballad), 30
Johnson, James Weldon, 26
Johnson, Robert, 30
Joplin, Janis, 80
jubilee songs, 26–27, 28

KDKA (radio station), 44
Keb' Mo', 52, 85
Kennedy, John F., 85
Kentucky, 51
KFFA (radio station), 45
King, B.B., 45
King Biscuit Time (radio program), 45
Kingston Trio (musical group), 65–66, 67, 69
klezmer music, 40
Knott, Sarah Gertrude, 32
Krauss, Alison, 85, 87

Land Where the Blues Began, The (Alan Lomax), 88–89
"Leave Her, Johnny" (ballad), 36
Ledbetter, Huddie (Lead Belly), 59, 60, 70, 87, 88
Lennon, John, 81
Library of Congress, 48, 49–51, 56, 59, 60, 89
Limeliters (musical group), 67, 79
lining out, 18
"Little Old Log Cabin in the Lane" (song), 44
Lobos, Los (band), 86
Lockwood, Robert Junior, 45
Lomax, Alan, 11, 25, 31, 39, 49–51, 59, 63, 81, 87, 88–89
Lomax, John A., 11, 37, 48, 49–51, 59
"Lord Rendal" (ballad), 16
Lornell, Kip, 41, 78
Louisiana, 32, 33, 52
Lovett, Lyle, 83
Lovin' Spoonful (musical group), 80
lullabies, 16, 21
lumberjacks, 36
Lummis, Charles, 48
lyric songs, 16

MacLeish, Archibald, 50–51
Macon, Uncle Dave, 45
"Maggie's Farm" (song), 74
Mahal, Taj, 85
"Mairi's Wedding" (reel), 13
Malone, Bill C., 72, 82
mandolin, 40

vocal song, 12, 15

"Wabash Cannonball, The" (song), 46
"Walk Right In" (song), 64
Wallace, Sippie, 83
Washington Square Park, 70
Waters, Muddy, 45, 52, 81, 88
Watson, Doc, 74
waulking songs, 16–17
Wayfarers (musical group), 67
Weavers (musical group), 57–58, 63, 66
Weissman, Dick, 77–78, 87, 89
Welch, Gillian, 84, 87
Welsh music, 15
Wesley, Charles, 27
western swing, 52–54
"Where Did You Sleep Last Night?" (song), 87
"Where Have All the Flowers Gone?" (song), 56

White, Josh, 63
White Top folk festival, 48–49
Wilco (band), 84, 87
"Wildwood Flower" (song), 46
Williams, Dar, 83
Williams, Hank, 45
Williams, Lucinda, 83
Williamson, Sonny Boy, II, 45
Wills, Bob, 52
"Will the Circle Be Unbroken" (song), 46
Wilson, Earl, 68
Winchester, Jesse, 83
work songs, 16–17, 26, 35–36
Works Progress Administration, 48
WSM (radio station), 45

Young, Neil, 80

Zimmerman, Robert. *See* Dylan, Bob

• Picture Credits •

• About the Author •

Adam Woog has written over forty books for adults, teens, and children. For Lucent Books, he has explored such subjects as Louis Armstrong, Anne Frank, Elvis Presley, sweatshops, Prohibition, and the New Deal. Woog lives with his wife and their daughter in Seattle, Washington.